Excel

ADVANCED SKILLS

ENGLISH

YEAR 1

AGES 6–7

GRAMMAR AND PUNCTUATION WORKBOOK

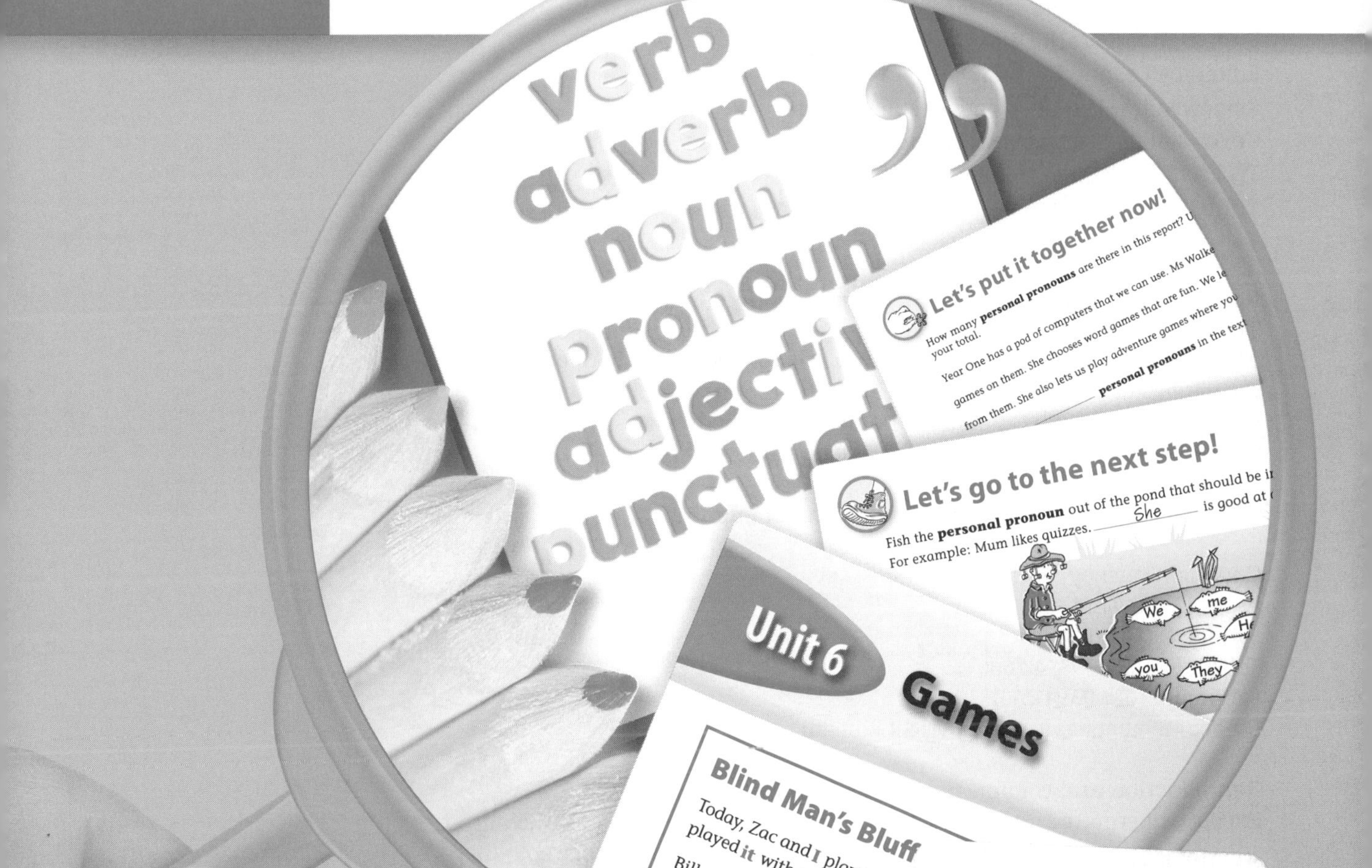

Get the Results You Want!

PASCAL PRESS

Donna Gibbs

Reprinted 2015, 2016, 2017, 2019, 2020, 2021, 2022

ISBN 978 1 74125 441 9

Pascal Press
PO Box 250
Glebe NSW 2037
(02) 8585 4050
www.pascalpress.com.au

Publisher: Vivienne Joannou
Project editor: Mark Dixon
Edited by Leanne Howard
Reviewed by Dale Little and Kristine Brown
Cover and page design by DiZign Pty Ltd
Typeset by lj Design (Julianne Billington)
Printed by Vivar Printing/Green Giant Press

Contents

To the student

This book explains the rules of grammar and punctuation that you need for Year 1.

Each unit focuses on two or more grammar rules. Before each rule is explained, there is a text that lets you see how the rule works in everyday writing. These texts are important as they are models of the different types of texts and will help you in your own writing. At the end of each unit there is also a short NAPLAN-style test that lets you see how well you have understood the grammar rules.

Most of the activities can be written in this book, but you will have to use your own paper for the writing activity at the end of each unit. I suggest you buy a notebook or folder for this. The writing activities are very important. The more you do, the faster your English will improve. If you are not sure how to write something, use the example texts as a model.

It is important that you work through this book from Unit 1 to the end. This will help you build your skills and become a more confident speaker and writer of English. Make sure that you understand the work in each unit before you go on to the next one. Remember to have a dictionary handy as you work through the book, and to ask for help if you need it. There is a glossary on page 85 that explains the grammatical terms used in the units.

I hope you enjoy reading the texts and doing all the activities.

Good luck!

Donna Gibbs

About this book

This book consists of 14 units, each covering one or more aspects of grammar or punctuation. Each unit is theme-based and contains two texts designed to introduce the grammatical features and to show students how they function in context. These are followed by detailed explanations of how and why the grammar features are used, as well as exercises that allow students to put the knowledge they have acquired into practice. As an aid to revision, there is a glossary at the end of the book that summarises the grammatical terms used in the units.

The exercises in the units are organised as follows:

Let's find them!

- These exercises require students to find examples of the grammatical feature in question in the texts. They are straightforward exercises designed to test recall.

Let's go to the next step!

- This set of exercises is more difficult, requiring students to apply the knowledge they have acquired.

Let's aim high now!

- These are challenging exercises, again requiring students to apply what they have learnt.

Let's put it all together now!

- This is an editing exercise designed to test the students' understanding of the material covered in the whole unit. It also acts as a revision exercise.

Let's have fun!

- Although this exercise is designed to be fun, it is also challenging. It reinforces the material learnt.

Let's have a test!

- This series of eight NAPLAN-style questions helps students revise for the NAPLAN Tests and also tests their knowledge of the material learnt in the unit as a whole. The questions are graded so that they increase in difficulty.

Let's write now!

- This activity encourages students to write their own text in which they use the grammar and punctuation they have learnt in the unit. The texts are based on the theme and types of texts featured in the unit.

Most of the exercises in this book consist of 5–6 questions, as we believe this gives students the practice they need to fully grasp the rules of grammar and punctuation.

Unit 1 Beginnings

Focus

Common nouns

Jack's diary

29th January

Dear Diary,
I saw my Year One **classroom** today. The **desks** and **chairs** were painted green. My desk was near the window. A box of pencils and a ruler were on my desk.
I saw some posters on the walls. There was a whiteboard too. A computer stood in the corner. When I clicked the mouse, the screen lit up. In the afternoon we sat on beanbags. We read books from the library. I think I will like my new classroom.
by Jack

This is a **diary entry**. Diary entries are daily events written about in a diary. Jack uses **common nouns** to name things when writing about his first day in Year One.

Common nouns name things; for example, **classroom**, **desks**, **chairs**.

Let's find them!

Find the **common nouns** in the text that name things.
For example: Jack's desk is near the ___window___.

1. Pencils and a ruler were on Jack's ______________________.
2. A ______________________ stood in the corner.
3. Jack clicked the ______________________.
4. The children sat on ______________________.
5. The children read ______________________.

Let's go to the next step!

Put the **common nouns** from the box into these sentences.

For example: I ruled a line with my ruler.

beanbag	computer	ruler	pencil	whiteboard	window

1. We used the new ______________________ to play games.
2. The teacher drew a picture on the ______________________.
3. I love sitting in this ______________________.
4. His desk was near the ______________________.
5. I wrote my name with a ______________________.

Let's aim high now!

Jim's sentences don't make any sense! Replace the underlined **common nouns** with one from the box.

For example: I sat on my <u>computer</u>. chair

wall	floor	chair	poster	whiteboard	bags

1. She wrote on the <u>paintbrush</u>. ______________________
2. The map was hanging on the <u>crayon</u>. ______________________
3. There was a <u>computer</u> pinned to the wall. ______________________
4. When the bell rang, they packed their <u>tables</u>. ______________________
5. I walked across the <u>map</u> to get to the door. ______________________

Our first excursion

Our **teacher** took us on our first excursion yesterday. We went to an animal sanctuary. I got a map from the caretaker.

First we saw some friendly **kangaroos**. Next we saw some koalas. They were high in the trees, eating gum leaves. Then we came to the wombats. The ranger told us that a baby wombat is as small as a jellybean!

The guide showed us a python. I think I saw a platypus but I'm not sure. I hope we can visit the animals again soon.

by Olga

This is a **recount**. Recounts tell about events that have happened. Olga uses **common nouns** to name the people and animals she saw on her excursion.

Common nouns name people and animals; for example, **teacher**, **kangaroos**.

Let's find them!

Find the **common nouns** naming people or animals that go in the spaces. The first one has been done for you.

1. The caretaker gave Olga a map.
2. The ______________________ were eating gum leaves.
3. A baby ______________________ is as small as a jellybean.
4. The ______________________ showed them a python.
5. Olga thinks she saw a ______________________.
6. Olga hopes to visit the ______________________ again.

Let's go to the next step!

Underline the **common nouns** that name animals in these sentences.
For example: I've read a book about a wombat.

1. The possum stared at me.
2. Bats like to hang upside down.
3. Bilbies have long ears.
4. Pythons live in caves and trees.
5. I saw a lizard that looked enormous!
6. Is that a snake in the grass?

Let's aim high now!

Underline the **common nouns** that name people in these sentences.
For example: My big sister took me to the animal sanctuary.

1. The zookeeper knows a lot about animals.
2. Her parents said she could have a pet.
3. Your friend said he saw a platypus.
4. The visitors bought their tickets at the gate.
5. Our teacher pointed to a joey.
6. The vet looked at the sick animal.

Let's put it together now!

Sort these **common nouns** into the correct columns. The first one in each column has been done for you.

koalas
house
kangaroos
gate
guide
lizards
vet
tree
wombats
driver
ticket
caretaker
cage
teacher
bilbies

Things	People	Animals
house	guide	koalas

Let's have fun!

In the picture of Jack's classroom below, draw a line from each **common noun** to its picture.

Let's have a test!

Tip!
Shade the circle next to the correct answer

1. Choose the common noun that names an animal.
   - ◯ leaves
   - ◯ snake
   - ◯ cage
   - ◯ tree

2. Choose the common noun that names a person.
   - ◯ feet
   - ◯ fence
   - ◯ gate
   - ◯ teacher

3. Choose the common noun that names a thing.
   - ◯ vet
   - ◯ koala
   - ◯ desk
   - ◯ helper

In questions 4–5, which common noun goes in the space?

4. The koala sat on the branch munching ____________________.
   - ◯ visitors
   - ◯ leaves
   - ◯ wallabies
   - ◯ houses

5. The ____________________ looked after the sick possum.
   - ◯ vet
   - ◯ artist
   - ◯ musician
   - ◯ singer

6. Which list of common nouns is a list of people?
   - ◯ bilby, bandicoot, wallaby
   - ◯ whiteboard, duster, pen
   - ◯ worker, cleaner, trainer
   - ◯ milk, juice, water

7. Which list of common nouns is a list of things?
   - ◯ table, chair, ruler
   - ◯ gorilla, lion, elephant
   - ◯ visitor, driver, leader
   - ◯ bat, bird, fish

8. Which is the common noun in this sentence?

   He pointed to a small, furry rabbit.

Let's write now!

Write a **diary entry** about a visit to an interesting place. Use **common nouns** to name the people, animals and things seen on your visit.

Unit 2 Holidays

More common nouns

A letter to Auntie Rosa

20th January

Dear Auntie Rosa,
It is school holidays now. We had a picnic by the **river** last week. I played with my new frisbee on the **oval**.
Mum and dad like taking us to the courts to play tennis. My brother loves riding his bike at the park.
My sister meets her friends in town. I like playing cricket in the backyard. Best of all, I like going to the beach. Hope you can visit us soon,
Love
Skye

This is a **letter**. Letters are messages in writing sent to another person. Skye uses **common nouns** to name the places that the family visits in the holidays.

Common nouns name places; for example, **river**, **oval**.

Let's find them!

Find the **common nouns** in the text that name places.
For example: Skye played with her new frisbee on the ___oval___.

1. Skye's brother rides his bike at the ______________.
2. Skye's sister meets her friends in ______________.
3. Skye likes to play cricket in the ______________.
4. Skye likes to go to the ______________ best of all.

Let's go to the next step!

Circle the **common nouns** that name places in these sentences.
For example: Mum went to the (office) today.

1. My dog is in the garden.
2. We start back at school next week.
3. We went to the supermarket.
4. We played football on the oval.
5. She likes swimming in the river.

Let's aim high now!

Put a **common noun**, naming a place, from the box into the spaces. The first one has been done for you.

cafe	pool	station	sea	park	postbox

1. Are you taking your snorkel to the ___pool___ today?
2. We rode our bikes at the ______________.
3. We are having a holiday by the ______________.
4. Eating in a ______________ is fun.
5. I posted my postcard in the ______________.
6. We get off the train at the next ______________.

Our island holiday

This year our **family** went away for the holidays. We had to leave our **dog** at **home**.

We went on an **aeroplane**. We landed on an island where we stayed for five days. There were three pools and I stayed in my swimmers most of the day. There were lots of children for me to play with.

On the third day, we bought snorkels. Then we had lessons in how to snorkel down at the beach.

When Dad was on the golf course he saw a snake in the bush. It was a pretty good holiday.

by Leon

This is another **recount**. Remember that recounts tell about events that have happened. Leon uses **common nouns** that name people, animals, places and things in telling about his family holiday.

Common nouns name people, animals, places and things; for example, **family**, **dog**, **home**, **aeroplane**.

Let's find them!

Find the **common nouns** in the text that go in the spaces.
For example: They landed on an ______ island ______.

1. Leon stayed in his ______________________ most of the day.
2. Leon had lots of ______________________ to play with.
3. They bought ______________________.
4. They had lessons at the ______________________.
5. Leon's Dad saw a ______________________.

Let's go to the next step!

Put a **common noun** from the box into the spaces. The first one has been done for you.

river	prize	friend	cards	pilot	boat

1. My mum won a ____prize____ for her christmas cake.
2. We travelled by ________ to our holiday.
3. She packed a deck of ________ in her suitcase.
4. The ________ of our plane was very tall.
5. We took a canoe on the ________.
6. Last year I took a ________ on holiday.

Let's aim high now!

Do the underlined **common nouns** name people, animals, places or things? Put the answer in the column. The first one has been done for you.

1. Some days we ate at a <u>cafe</u>.
2. We had <u>fruit</u> for breakfast.
3. Are you going to the <u>mountains</u> for your holiday?
4. We had to leave our dog at the <u>kennels</u>.
5. We let our <u>dog</u> come inside the caravan.
6. She gave her <u>friends</u> a ticket.
7. Don't forget to take your <u>towel</u> and swimmers on your holiday.

Common noun	People, animals, places or things?
cafe	place
fruit	
mountains	
kennels	
dog	
friend	
towel	

Let's put it together now!

Sort these **common nouns** into the correct columns. The first one in each column has been done for you.

photo	kennels	bus	woman
girl	dog	beach	bag
motel	boy	child	uncle
rabbit	postcard	snake	cat
shops	birds	suitcase	cattery

People	Animals	Places	Things
girl	rabbit	motel	photo

Let's have fun!

The clues will help you work out the **common nouns** that complete this puzzle.

ACROSS

1. You can swim in this.
3. A train driver drives this.
4. You can take a canoe on this.
5. There is sand and sea here.
7. A tram driver drives this.

DOWN

1. You can fly in this.
2. This is a place to stay that rhymes with hotel.
6. Families drive in this.

		1							2	
3										
						4				
	5			6						
			7							

Let's have a test!

1. Which list of common nouns is a list of people?
   - ◯ tower, bridge, building
   - ◯ brother, mother, father
   - ◯ cat, dog, horse
   - ◯ park, stream, playground

2. Which list of common nouns is a list of animals?
   - ◯ chemist, doctor, grocer
   - ◯ garden, backyard, oval
   - ◯ hen, fox, rooster
   - ◯ box, washbag, ticket

3. Which list of common nouns is a list of things?
   - ◯ toys, games, puzzles
   - ◯ cows, goats, sheep
   - ◯ rabbits, goats, horses
   - ◯ man, woman, teacher

4. Which list of common nouns is a list of places?
   - ◯ friend, enemy, relative
   - ◯ river, beach, mountains
   - ◯ money, suitcase, passport
   - ◯ mouse, chicken, rooster

5. Which word is a common noun that names a thing?

   We caught a bus to the city.

6. Which word is a common noun that names a person?

   The guide showed us the animals.

7. Which word is a common noun that names a place?

   My family is staying at a motel.

8. Which sentence does **not** have a common noun?
   - ◯ They caught a train to the city.
   - ◯ He was flown by helicopter to the hospital.
   - ◯ We flew in an aeroplane to the seaside.
   - ◯ You can't go in there because it is closed.

Let's write now!

Write a **recount** about a holiday you have had. Use **common nouns** to name the people, animals, places and things you saw.

Unit 3 Family time

★ Focus

Proper nouns; capital letters

My family

We are the **Kanes**. There are six of us. My father is Robert Kane. He is forty-three years old. My mother is Louisa Kane. She is forty-one years old.

There are four children. The oldest are the twins called Bo and Jo. They are ten years old. Then comes Amy. She is eight. My name is Simon. I am the youngest in the Kane family. I am nearly six. **Butch** is our dog. We also have a cat called Popo, and a canary called Tweet.

by Simon

This is an **information report**. Information reports give information about a subject. Simon uses **proper nouns** to name each member of the Kane family.

Proper nouns name particular people or animals. They always have **capital letters**; for example, **Kanes**, **Butch**.

Let's find them!

Find the **proper noun(s)** in the text that go in the spaces.
For example: Simon's father is named ____Robert Kane____.

1. Simon's mother is named ______________________.
2. One twin is named ______________________.
3. The other twin is named ______________________.
4. The Kane's cat is named ______________________.
5. The Kane's canary is named ______________________.

Tip! When there is more than one word that is part of the name, each word has a **capital letter**; for example, **Robert Kane**.

Let's go to the next step!

Circle the **proper nouns** that name people or animals in the sentences below.
For example: Is Betty older than you are?

1. Snowball, my fluffy dog, is very cuddly.
2. Our family doctor is named Dr Knight.
3. The Wongs have moved to a new house.
4. Mr Ho is our dentist.
5. Mary wants to be a doctor.

Let's aim high now!

The **proper nouns** in these sentences have lost their **capital letters**. Rewrite the sentences correctly.
For example: mr power married ms light. Mr Power married Ms Light.

1. She phoned dr knight. ______________________
2. Did you see our prime minister? ______________________
3. Our family watches donald duck. ______________________
4. Auntie jo gave me a present. ______________________
5. We will visit uncle julian soon. ______________________

From: Amy Kane
Subject: Can't wait
Date: 12th June
To: Julian King, <julianking@backstop.com.au>

Hi Uncle Julian,

Thank you for saying you will meet us at the airport at **Kuala Lumpur** in Malaysia. We can't wait to see you.

We are staying in some units called Desa Kiara. We hope to visit the Twin Towers. Jo said it is the tallest building in the world. The other place I'd like to visit is the Kuala Lumpur Bird Park.

Do you think Mandy and Tommy will play **Monopoly** and Snakes and Ladders with me? Mum has packed some Vegemite to bring you. She said it is hard to find it in Malaysia.

Love

Amy xx

This is an **email**. Emails are electronic messages. Amy uses **proper nouns** in her email to name particular places and things.

Proper nouns name particular places (e.g. **Kuala Lumpur**) or things (e.g. **Monopoly**).

Let's find them!

Find the **proper noun(s)** in the text that name particular places and things.

For example: the name of a country ___Malaysia___

Tip!

Remember: if there is more than one word in the name, each word has a **capital letter**; for example, **Uncle Julian**.

1. the name of the units where the family will stay ______________________
2. the name of a very tall building ______________________
3. the name of Uncle Julian's daughter starting with *M* ______________________
4. the name of a game starting with *S* ______________________
5. the name of something you spread on toast ______________________

Let's go to the next step!

Circle the **proper nouns** that name particular places or things.
For example: I hope we can visit the (Gold Coast).

1. My brother goes to the movies in Avalon.
2. Our family loves to eat at Chinatown.
3. Dad bought a Mazda that fits all the family.
4. My friend said she saw Ayers Rock.
5. We went on the Manly Ferry.

Let's aim high now!

The **proper nouns** in these sentences are underlined. Do they name places or things?
For example: Our next holiday will be at Ayers Rock. ______place______

1. You can see interesting plants in the Daintree National Park. ________________
2. My dad bought a new Holden. ________________
3. We went to New Zealand for a week last year. ________________
4. Sometimes we have Vegemite on toast. ________________
5. I have never seen the Pacific Ocean. ________________
6. The space ship flew towards Mars. ________________

Let's put it together now!

Amy has forgotten to give the **proper nouns** their capital letters in her report about the Gold Coast. Circle her mistakes.

The gold coast is a good place for a holiday in australia. At sea world you can see marine animals. You can see sharks swimming at shark bay. You can go to the carrara markets. Children can have their faces painted there. There is always something to do at the gold coast.

How many **capital letters** did you add? Write the number below.

Let's have fun!

Draw a picture in the box of you and your family celebrating a birthday together. Name the people in your picture: for example, Amy Kane, Louisa Kane.

Let's have a test!

In questions 1–2, which words in the sentences are proper nouns?

1. We saw some coral in Queensland.

2. I hope our family has a holiday in Darwin.

3. Which proper noun goes in the space?
   Will you leave ______________ in the kennels?
   - Kleenex
   - Mr Brown
   - Spot
   - Peter Rabbit

In questions 4–5, which sentence has a proper noun?

4. - Our family loves barbeques.
   - Our family caught a tram.
   - Our family went to Ayers Rock.
   - Everyone in our family has a cold.

5. - I don't think he should be famous.
   - I would not like to be famous.
   - We like watching famous people on television.
   - The Sydney Harbour Bridge is famous.

6. Which list of proper nouns names places?
   - Skippy Park, Sea World, Perth
   - Monday, Tuesday, Wednesday
   - Spot, Whiskers, Tweet
   - May, July, September

7. Which list of proper nouns names people?
   - Perth, Sydney, Hobart
   - Sally, Tomoko, Amy
   - Collins Street, George Street, Rundle Street
   - Monopoly, Snakes and Ladders, Snap

8. Which of these proper nouns has been written **incorrectly**?
   - Twin Towers
   - Great Barrier Reef
   - australia
   - Chinatown

Let's write now!

Write an **email** to a family friend who is coming to visit you. Use **proper nouns** to tell them about places to visit and people to see.

Unit 4 Seasons

Focus

Adjectives

Winter

A **chilly** frost bites my **little**, **pink** nose!
Icy winds bruise my tiny, pink toes.
Brrrr. It's cold.
I dream of a fire, cosy and warm,
a place of escape
from this terrible storm.
Brrrr. It's cold.
If only my scarf, so woolly and red,
was wrapped around my freezing, cold head.
If only my mac was over my back,
If only.
Brrrr. It's cold.
by Oliver

This is a **description** in the form of a poem. Descriptions help us form pictures in our mind. In this poem, Oliver uses **adjectives** to add meaning to nouns in order to describe people, places and things in winter.

An **adjective** is a word that adds meaning to a noun; for example, **chilly** (frost), **little**, **pink** (nose).

Let's find them!

Tip!
There are two **adjectives** in some answers.

Find the **adjective(s)** in the poem that describe the following.
For example: the winds ___icy___

1. Oliver's toes ______________________
2. the fire Oliver dreams about ______________________
3. the storm ______________________
4. Oliver's scarf ______________________
5. Oliver's head ______________________

Let's go to the next step!

Circle the **adjective** in the sentence that tells more about the underlined noun.
For example: That was a (heavy) <u>snowfall</u>.

1. The rain made big <u>puddles</u>.
2. It was a very foggy <u>morning</u>.
3. He made a jolly <u>snowman</u>.
4. I hope we have a log <u>fire</u>.
5. You can expect cold <u>weather</u>.
6. I can see some blue <u>sky</u>.

Let's aim high now!

There is an **adjective** in each sentence. Write it on the lines.
For example: January is a hot month. ______hot______

1. Winter lasts for three months. ____________________
2. Sometimes there are sunny days in winter. ____________________
3. There was black ice on the road. ____________________
4. Snakes often sleep in cold weather. ____________________
5. I have a woolly scarf. ____________________
6. There was slippery ice on the road. ____________________

Summer

Summer has **hot** days, **blue** skies and **fluffy**, **white** clouds. Smells of sunscreen and salty air remind me of summer.

I love having bare feet. I love eating freezing iceblocks that melt all over me! I love the warm sun on my body.

We swim at the beach and build wobbly sandcastles. There are swooping seagulls, scuttling crabs and fish and chips for dinner. Summer is the best season.

by Hugo

This is another **description**. Hugo uses **adjectives** to add meaning to the nouns he uses to describe people, places and things in summer.

Remember that an **adjective** is a describing word that adds meaning to a noun; for example, **hot** (days), **blue** (skies), **fluffy**, **white** (clouds).

Let's find them!

Find eight more **adjectives** in the text that describe nouns. The first one has been done for you.

1. salty
2. ______
3. ______
4. ______
5. ______
6. ______
7. ______
8. ______

Let's go to the next step!

These sentences don't make much sense! Choose an **adjective** from the box to replace the one that is underlined.

For example: The cold sun warmed us up. hot

outdoor	Sunny	burning	summer	wet	hot	high

1. Rainy days are good for building sandcastles. ____________
2. We go to the beach for our winter holiday. ____________
3. We play lots of indoor sports in summer. ____________
4. That low temperature means summer is here. ____________
5. The freezing sand scorched my feet. ____________
6. I have dry hair from my swim. ____________

Let's aim high now!

Circle the **adjective** and underline the noun it describes in these sentences.

For example: I saw a (tiny) crab under the rock.

1. That cheeky seagull stole my sandwich.
2. She has new swimmers.
3. There was a dead fish on the shore.
4. My dog paddles in shallow water.
5. Dad caught a small crab

Let's put it together now!

Some **adjectives** in this poem are scrambled. Write the correct spelling in the spaces.

Autumn Leaves

dRe leaves, ownbr leaves, georan leaves
Falling slowly to the hard ground
neO leaf, then rethe, then oufr leaves, flutter down
They gather into deep piles in the eygr gutter
Now I come and kick them about,
The crunchy leaves of autumn.

Autumn Leaves

____________ leaves, ____________ leaves, ____________ leaves

Falling slowly to the hard ground

____________ leaf, then ____________, then ____________ leaves, flutter down

They gather into deep piles in the ____________ gutter

Now I come and kick them about,

The crunchy leaves of autumn.

Let's have fun!

Match these to the correct picture by drawing a line to connect them. The first one has been done for you.

- cheerful snowman
- tiny crab
- snowy mountain
- huge wave
- striped umbrella
- tall sandcastle
- spotted beach ball
- shady sunhat

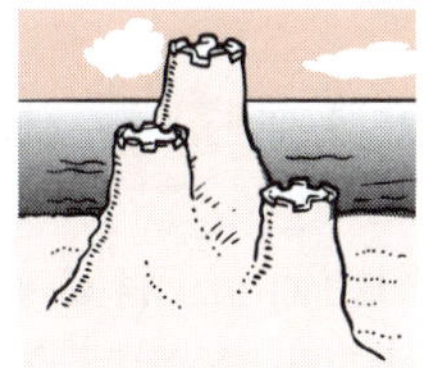

Let's have a test!

In questions 1–2, which sentence has an adjective?

1. ◯ I went for a walk.
   ◯ It was a cold day.
   ◯ I walked in the snow.
   ◯ I sat by the fire.

2. ◯ It was a sunny day.
   ◯ I sat in the shade.
   ◯ I put on my hat.
   ◯ I kept out of the sun.

In questions 3–6, which word is the adjective?

3. Susie has new sunglasses.

4. I bought Ashley a red iceblock.

5. During the storm there was flashing lightning.

6. The waves splashed up onto the large rocks.

In questions 7–8, which adjective goes in the space?

7. In winter we keep our hands warm by wearing ____________ gloves.
   ◯ rubber ◯ woolly
   ◯ plastic ◯ paper

8. My hat keeps the ____________ sun out of my eyes.
   ◯ crazy ◯ chilly
   ◯ good ◯ bright

Let's write now!

Write a short **descriptive** poem about your favourite time of the year. Use **adjectives** to bring your poem to life.

Unit 5 Animals

Focus
Singular and plural nouns

This is another **information report**. The report uses **singular** and **plural nouns** in giving information about dolphins.

Dolphins

Dolphins are mammals. They have a large brain. They have small ears but they can hear very well. Their jaws are shaped like beaks. Some dolphins have up to 250 teeth.

On the high part of a dolphin's head, there is a blowhole. The **dolphin** can close the blowhole to make it watertight.

Dolphins can swim very quickly. Sometimes they leap out of the water. They are playful animals.

Common nouns can be counted. A **singular noun** names one person, animal, place or thing; for example, **dolphin**. A **plural noun** names more than one; for example, **dolphins**.

Let's find them!

Find the **plural nouns** in the text that go in the spaces.
For example: Dolphins are ______mammals______.

1. Dolphins have small ____________________.
2. Their jaws are like ____________________.
3. Some dolphins have up to 250 ____________________.

Find the **singular nouns** in the text that go in the spaces.

4. Dolphins have a large ____________________.
5. A dolphin has a ____________________ on its head.
6. Dolphins can leap out of the ____________________.

Let's go to the next step!

These **nouns** are **plural**. Write the word for the **singular**. The first one has been done for you.

1. penguins ______ penguin ______
2. lions ____________________
3. whales ____________________
4. tigers ____________________
5. sharks ____________________

These **nouns** are **singular**. They name one of each thing. Write their **plurals**.

6. dolphin ____________________
7. seal ____________________
8. giraffe ____________________
9. monkey ____________________
10. animal ____________________

Let's aim high now!

Do you need a **singular** or a **plural noun** to complete these sentences? Underline the correct choice.

For example: Zoo/Zoos are places where animals are kept.

1. A dolphin/dolphins is a playful animal.
2. Sharks have fin/fins.
3. Penguins have flipper/flippers.
4. A dolphin is a mammal/mammals.
5. Are seal/seals good swimmers?
6. She saw a seahorse/seahorses.

From: Aaron Mohan
Subject: Zoos
Date: 7th June
To: John Mohan <johntmohan@network.com>

Hi Uncle John

Thanks for your email from London. I liked the **pictures** of the baby penguins with their mother.

We are studying zoos at school. I have learned about **deer** and fish this week. For homework, we had to draw their pictures. I watched some DVDs about animals with the **children** in my class.

Some men and women who work at the zoo came to talk to our class about caring for the animals. Maybe I'll work in a zoo when I grow up!

Love
Aaron

This is an **email**. Remember that emails are electronic messages. In his email to Uncle John, Aaron uses **singular** and **plural nouns** to tell what he has learned about animals in zoos.

Remember that many **singular nouns** add *s* or *es* to make them **plural** (e.g. **picture → pictures**). Some nouns are made plural in different ways. For example:

- Some change their form (e.g. **child → children**).
- Some stay the same (e.g. **deer** is both **singular** and **plural**).

Let's find them!

Find the **plural nouns** in the text that answer these questions.
For example: Which animals in the pictures did Aaron like? penguins

1. Which topic is Aaron studying? ______
2. What animals did Aaron learn about (other than the example)? ______
3. What did the class draw for homework? ______
4. What were the DVDs about? ______
5. Who talked to the class? ______ and ______

Let's go to the next step!

Write the **plural nouns** in the column. The first one has been done for you.

Singular	Plural
one tiger	two tigers
one elephant	two
one deer	two
one bird	two
one monkey	two
one man	two
one child	two

Let's aim high now!

Are the underlined **nouns singular** or **plural**?
For example: Baby monkeys look very sweet. plural

1. A giraffe has a very long neck. ______
2. The children went to the zoo. ______
3. I watched a film about animals. ______
4. A seal is a mammal. ______
5. I love watching birds. ______
6. The deer hid from us as she was shy. ______

Let's put it together now!

Put circles around the **singular nouns** and underline the **plural nouns** in the text below. The first one has been done for you.

Tip! There are three **singular nouns** and seven **plural nouns**.

We bought our tickets at the gate.

We rushed into the zoo to see the animals.

We saw lions prowling around.

Next came the monkeys who made us laugh. We loved the giraffes. They had long necks and soft eyes. What a good day we had!

Let's have fun!

There are five **plural nouns** hiding in this puzzle: lions, giraffes, tigers, zoos and monkeys. Draw a coloured line around each plural noun when you find it.

c	r	b	o	q	o	z	t
l	i	o	n	s	t	o	i
s	m	e	r	f	g	o	g
u	m	p	o	h	e	s	e
m	o	n	k	e	y	s	r
s	s	o	r	e	f	t	s
g	i	r	a	f	f	e	s
h	o	s	p	a	n	z	j

Let's have a test!

In questions 1–2, which sentence contains a singular noun?

1. ◯ I fed the elephants. ◯ Did you see those large elephants? ◯ Those elephants are very large. ◯ That elephant is very large.

2. ◯ The crocodile snapped his jaws. ◯ Some crocodiles live in rivers. ◯ Crocodiles move quickly. ◯ Crocodiles have long jaws.

In questions 3–4, which sentence contains a plural noun?

3. ◯ I saw a dolphin in the sea. ◯ I saw a whale in the sea. ◯ I saw a penguin on the beach. ◯ Did you see any dolphins?

4. ◯ The lion belongs to the cat family. ◯ A male lion has a big mane. ◯ Male and female lions look different. ◯ A female lion is called a lioness.

5. Which is the singular noun in this sentence?

   She looked at photos of lions and tigers on her computer.

6. Which is the plural noun in this sentence?

   She gave the geese a bucket of food.

In questions 7–8, which sentence has a plural noun spelt **incorrectly**?

7. ◯ There are gorillas in the zoo. ◯ There are hippos in the zoo. ◯ There are monkeyes in the zoo. ◯ There are deer in the zoo.

8. ◯ We watched the dolphins leap. ◯ We watched the seales sunbake. ◯ We watched the penguins waddle. ◯ We watched the sharks swim.

Let's write now!

Write a short **information report** about another animal who lives in the sea. Take care to use **singular** and **plural nouns** correctly.

Unit 6 Games

Focus

Personal pronouns

Blind Man's Bluff

Today, Zac and **I** played a game. Bill, Jane and Portia played **it** with us.

Bill was blindfolded. He had to turn around three times. Jane counted to ten. We all ran away and hid.

Bill called out 'Here I come,' in a scary voice.

Portia, Jane and I kept really quiet, but Zac tripped over a stone. Bill knew where to find him then. Zac was next to put on the blindfold.

So far I haven't been caught out!

by Mark

This is a **recount**. Remember that recounts tell you about events that have happened. Mark uses **personal pronouns** to stand for nouns as he tells about playing a game with his friends.

Personal pronouns are words that are used to stand for nouns. This saves repeating nouns; for example, **I** stands for **Mark**; **it** stands for **game**.

Let's find them!

Find seven more **personal pronouns** that stand for nouns in the text. The first one has been done for you.

Tip!

The **personal pronouns** are **I**, **me**, **you**, **he**, **him**, **she**, **her**, **it**, **we**, **us**, **you**, **they** and **them**.

1. us
2. ______
3. ______
4. ______
5. ______
6. ______
7. ______

Let's go to the next step!

Circle the **personal pronouns** that stand for the underlined nouns in these sentences.
For example: My soccer boots were dirty so I cleaned (them).

1. Your team is good and it will win.
2. Mum and Dad went out and they bought a card game.
3. Jane's t-shirt is red and she wears it to play basketball.
4. Bill has a white cap he wears at cricket.
5. Her goggles don't fit, so Skye won't wear them.
6. Tom's football is gone and he can't find it.

Let's aim high now!

Underline the nouns and circle the **personal pronouns** that stand for them in these sentences.
For example: We play Snap because (it) is such fun.

1. He is good at games and always wins them.
2. Did Sally tell you that she can't play today?
3. Dad said he would watch us play cricket.
4. Please keep my bat until I need it.
5. She lost some puzzle pieces but then she found them.
6. Ella chased him and then he chased her.

Playing Jacks

I asked my Gran about games people played in the olden days. **She** said they liked to play a game called Jacks.

Gran said she made the jacks from the knuckles of lamb shank bones. When they were washed and painted they were ready to use.

She threw five jacks into the air. She had to catch one jack on the back of her hand, throw it up, and catch it again. Then she did that with two jacks, and so on. By the end, she had to catch all five of them.

I would like to try that game. Before I play it, we'll need to have shanks for dinner.

by Charlotte

This is another **recount**. Charlotte uses **personal pronouns** to stand for nouns as she tells how her Gran played Jacks.

Remember that **personal pronouns** are words used to stand for nouns. This saves repeating nouns; for example, **I** stands for **Charlotte**; **She** stands for **Gran**.

Let's find them!

Find these **personal pronoun(s)** in the text. The first one has been done for you.

1. Which pronouns stand for the noun *Gran*? she and her
2. Which pronoun stands for the noun *knuckles*? ______
3. Which pronoun stands for (one) *jack*? ______
4. Which pronoun stands for (all five of the) *jacks*? ______
5. Which pronoun stands for the noun *Charlotte*? ______
6. Which pronoun stands for the noun *game*? ______

Let's go to the next step!

Fish the **personal pronoun** out of the pond that should be in these sentences.
For example: Mum likes quizzes. ___She___ is good at answering them.

1. Dad likes golf. ______________ plays on Saturdays.
2. I like computer games. ______________ always beat myself!
3. Uncle Jo gave ______________ Scrabble for my birthday.
4. Sam and Sal play cards with us. ______________ often beat me.
5. Gran and I are good at Jacks. ______________ play every day.
6. Can you play Snap? Will ______________ play it with me?

Let's aim high now!

Which **personal pronoun** from the box stands for the noun(s) in brackets?
For example: I played (Fish) with my friend. ___it___

her	we	them	he	She	it	him

1. She gave (John and Jim) new football boots. ______________
2. Can (Sally and I) have a turn? ______________
3. (Scarlet) wants to play with us. ______________
4. I asked if (James) wanted a turn. ______________
5. Give (Nick) a turn after you've had yours. ______________

Let's put it together now!

How many **personal pronouns** are there in this report? Underline them and write your total.

Year One has a pod of computers that we can use. Ms Walker lets us play games on them. She chooses word games that are fun. We learn about words from them. She also lets us play adventure games where you find lost people.

There are ______________ personal pronouns in the text.

Let's have fun!

Solve this crossword by choosing a **personal pronoun** that rhymes with the word in the clue.

1	2		3		4		5		
					6				

Across

A personal pronoun that:

1 rhymes with *stay*

5 rhymes with *sea*

6 rhymes with *flea*

Down

A personal pronoun that:

2 rhymes with *tea*

3 rhymes with *shoe*

4 rhymes with *stem*

Let's have a test!

In questions 1–2, which word is the personal pronoun in each sentence?

1. I threw the ball to Jeremy.

2. Tiddlywinks is a game we like to play.

In questions 3–4, which sentence has a personal pronoun?

3.
- ◯ The team kicked three goals.
- ◯ They kicked three goals.
- ◯ How many goals were kicked?
- ◯ Three goals were kicked.

4.
- ◯ Card games are fun.
- ◯ There are lots of card games.
- ◯ Snap is a good card game.
- ◯ She likes playing card games.

In questions 5–6, which personal pronoun is needed to complete each sentence?

5. I heard that ______________ are good at rounders.
- ◯ I
- ◯ me
- ◯ you
- ◯ him

6. John asked me to hit the ball to ______________.
- ◯ me
- ◯ she
- ◯ him
- ◯ I

In questions 7–8, which sentence does not contain a personal pronoun?

7.
- ◯ Can you play Snap?
- ◯ Is Snap more fun than Fish?
- ◯ I am good at playing Fish.
- ◯ They played Snap together.

8.
- ◯ Gran used to play Jacks when she was young.
- ◯ Have you practised throwing the ball?
- ◯ I love to play hopscotch.
- ◯ Bill likes to play Blindman's Bluff.

Let's write now!

Write a **recount** about a game you have played. Use **personal pronouns** to stand for nouns where it saves repeating them.

Unit 7 Cooking

Focus

Doing verbs

Cooking sausage rolls

Yesterday I **cooked** sausage rolls for our school picnic. I **shopped** for sausage meat, flour and milk.

Mum helped me spread the pastry. She helped me chop some onions. I mixed the onions with the meat. Then I rolled the meat into a snake shape. I covered the 'snake' with pastry. Next I cut it into small pieces.

I put the small pieces on a tray and into the oven at 180 degrees. After fifteen minutes, they turned golden brown. Yum!

My cat **came** and rubbed against my legs. I know what she wanted!

by Hans

This is another **recount**. It uses **doing verbs** to tell what Hans did when he cooked sausage rolls.

Doing verbs show what people, animals or things do; for example, **cooked**, **shopped**, **came**.

Let's find them!

Find the **doing verbs** in the text.

For example: What did Mum help Hans do with the pastry? spread

1. What did Mum help Hans do with the onions? ____________
2. What did Hans do to make the meat a snake shape? ____________
3. What did Hans do to make the snake into small pieces? ____________
4. What did Hans do with the small pieces? ____________
5. What did the cat do against Hans's legs? ____________

Let's go to the next step!

Choose a **doing verb** from the box to complete each sentence. The first one has been done for you.

add	mash	barbecued	drink	chop	sprinkle	make

1. You need to ______chop______ the onions into small pieces.
2. Did you ____________ salt and pepper on the meat?
3. If you ____________ that much sugar, it will be too sweet.
4. Jelly is an easy recipe to ____________.
5. He ____________ the chops and sausages.
6. I like to ____________ the potatoes.
7. Are you going to ____________ your hot chocolate?

Let's aim high now!

Choose a **doing verb** from the box to match each group below.
For example: grill, boil, ______bake______

chew	bake	freeze	slice	stir	sip

1. cut, chop, ____________
2. drink, swallow, ____________
3. whip, mix, ____________
4. heat, cool, ____________
5. eat, gobble, ____________

Making fruit jelly

Ingredients

1 packet jelly

1 cup boiling water

200 ml fruit juice

1 can peach slices

Method

Open the packet of jelly and **empty** the jelly crystals into a bowl.

Boil the kettle and fill a jug with 1 cup of water.

Slowly add the boiling water to the jelly crystals. Stir carefully.

Open the can of peaches and pour 200 ml of juice and fruit into the jug. Add to the jelly mixture.

Place in fridge for 4 hours or more.

Delicious! Pat yourself on the back.

This is a set of **instructions**. The instructions use **doing verbs** to explain how to make fruit jelly.

Remember that **doing verbs** show what people, animals or things do; for example, **open** (the packet of jelly), **empty** (the jelly crystals).

Let's find them!

Circle the **doing verbs** in the parts of the text repeated below.

For example: (Boil) the kettle and (fill) a jug with one cup of water.

Tip! There is more than one **doing verb** in some of these.

1. Slowly add the boiling water to the jelly crystals. Stir carefully.
2. Open the can of peaches and pour 200 ml of juice and fruit into the jug. Add to the jelly mixture.
3. Place in fridge for 4 hours or more.
4. Delicious! Pat yourself on the back.

Let's go to the next step!

Choose a **doing verb** from the box to complete these sentences. The first one has been done for you.

hurried	peeled	ate	bought	grew	went	learned

1. I peeled the potatoes with a potato peeler.
2. We ______________ to a cafe for lunch.
3. I ______________ a large plate of macaroni.
4. Grandpa ______________ lettuces last year.
5. We ______________ home for dinner.
6. My brother ______________ to cook biscuits.
7. Dad ______________ lamb to make kebabs.

Let's aim high now!

What a muddle! These sentences have the wrong doing verbs. Circle the incorrect **doing verb**, then rewrite the sentence with the correct verb from the box.
For example: My sister sang the dinner. My sister cooked the dinner.

whipped	cooked	washed	ate	patted	drank

1. William drank his spaghetti. ______________
2. I sprinkled the cream. ______________
3. She ate the tablecloth. ______________
4. They chopped the lemonade. ______________
5. He swallowed his back. ______________

Let's put it together now!

Fill in the missing words in the clues to solve this crossword. They are all **doing verbs**; the first and last letters are given to help you with the answers.

ACROSS

1. She c __ t the pastry with a knife.
3. You c __ __ k eggs in a pan on the stove.
4. I will s __ __ __ e the apples for the pie.
5. I e __ t breakfast at home every day.

DOWN

1. Mum said I could c __ __ p the onions.
2. I love the t __ __ __ e of yoghurt.

1		2		3			
		4					
		5					

Let's have fun!

Unscramble the **doing verbs** in these sentences.
For example: She ntew to the shops to buy milk. went

1. I ximde the flour and water for the damper. ______
2. Dad kocode the chops and sausages. ______
3. Henry dmae some red jelly. ______
4. We detrnu the oven up to 180 degrees. ______
5. I deloib the kettle. ______

Let's have a test!

In questions 1–2, which word is a doing verb in the sentence?

1 Tom cooked eggs for lunch.

○ Tom ○ cooked ○ eggs ○ lunch

2 After dinner, we dried the dishes.

○ After ○ dinner ○ dried ○ dishes

In questions 3–4, which sentence has a doing verb?

3
- ○ Are you there?
- ○ I am at home.
- ○ He ran home.
- ○ He has a big house.

4
- ○ The dog was in his kennel.
- ○ The dog was hungry.
- ○ Do you have a dog?
- ○ The dog buried his bone.

5 Which doing verb goes in the space?

She ______________________ the milk and flour together.

○ sprinkled ○ bounced ○ mixed ○ rolled

6 Which of the following is a list of doing verbs?
- ○ has, had, have
- ○ was, were, will
- ○ is, am, are
- ○ cook, eat, chop

In questions 7–8, which sentence does **not** have a doing verb?

7
- ○ She poured the milk into the jug.
- ○ Is the milk in the jug?
- ○ She put the milk into the jug.
- ○ May I drink that milk in the jug?

8
- ○ Drink up your hot chocolate, please.
- ○ He made her some hot chocolate.
- ○ Here is your hot chocolate.
- ○ I heated some hot chocolate.

Let's write now!

Write a **recount** about something you have enjoyed doing such as making something or playing a game. Use **doing verbs** to explain what you did.

Unit 8 Life on the farm

Focus
Saying verbs

Feeding time

"Can I feed the baby lamb now?" **asked** Samantha.

"But I want a turn," **complained** Josh.

"The lamb has to be fed every three hours," said Mrs Chew. "You can both have turns."

"The milk is ready. Can I go first?" asked Samantha.

"That's not fair!" cried Josh.

"It is so!" shouted Samantha.

"Children," groaned Mrs Chew. "Stop! You'll frighten the poor baby lamb."

"Baaaaa," agreed the lamb.

This is a **narrative**. Remember that narratives tell a story. This narrative uses **saying verbs** to express the different ways characters say things in the story.

Saying verbs express different ways people say things; for example, **asked**, **complained**.

Let's find them!

Find six more **saying verbs** in the story and write them on the lines below. The first one has been done for you.

1. 

2. ______
3. ______
4. ______
5. ______
6. ______

Let's go to the next step!

Underline the **saying verbs** in these sentences.
For example: "Why can't I have a turn?" moaned Samantha.

1. "There's a fox near the chickens," yelled Su Lin.
2. "I have no eggs left," sighed Mrs Chew.
3. "We need new fences," replied Mr Chew.
4. "Don't go near the dam," called her mother.
5. "Have you fed your horse?" I asked.
6. "You could borrow my tractor," he suggested.

Let's aim high now!

Choose a **saying verb** from the box for each sentence. The first one has been done for you.

grumbled   asked   warned   said   sang   whispered   begged

1. "Old MacDonald had a farm," ______sang______ the children.
2. "Do not go near that bull," ____________________ the farmer.
3. "I don't want to milk the cows," ____________________ Josh.
4. "It was very noisy in the farmyard," ____________________ the farmer.
5. "Please, please, can I collect the eggs," she ____________________.
6. "Shhh. You'll wake the lamb," ____________________ Mrs Chew.
7. "Have you seen the movie called *Babe*?" I ____________________.

Who's boss?

"I am boss of this farm," **barked** the dog.

"You are not," **whinnied** the horse. "I am."

"No way," mooed the cow. "It's me."

"We are the bosses," quacked the ducks.

"What about us?" chirped the chicks.

"You silly animals," crowed the rooster. "I am the boss of you all."

"No you're not," cackled the hens.

"What's all this noise?" asked the farmer. "Who wants their dinner?"

"We do," the animals replied, and not another sound was heard in the farmyard that night.

This is another **narrative**. It uses **saying verbs** to express different ways animals say things in the story.

Saying verbs express different ways animals 'say' things; for example, **barked**, **whinnied**.

Let's find them!

Find seven more **saying verbs** in the story and write them on the lines below. The first one has been done for you.

1. mooed
2. __________
3. __________
4. __________
5. __________
6. __________
7. __________

Let's go to the next step!

Circle the **saying verbs** in these sentences.
For example: "I am ready to be milked," bleated the goat.

1. "You are in my way," oinked the pig.
2. "I am off to round up sheep," barked the dog.
3. "Have you seen my mum?" quacked the duckling.
4. "I am hungry," mooed the cow.
5. "I just laid my first egg," clucked the hen.
6. "I am giving donkey rides today," brayed the donkey.

Let's aim high now!

Choose a **saying verb** from the box for each sentence. The first one has been done for you.

bleated	cooed	tweeted	neighed	brayed	oinked	squeaked

1. "Good morning," ____cooed____ the pigeons.
2. "Hello," ________________ the birds.
3. "How do you do?" ________________ the horses.
4. "Good afternoon," ________________ the donkeys.
5. "Good day," ________________ the pigs.
6. "Good evening," ________________ the mice.
7. "Good night," ________________ the goat.

Let's put it together now!

Sort the list of **saying verbs** from the box into the columns. The first one in each column has been done for you.

buzzed	hooted	agreed	honked
asked	whispered	cheeped	shouted
bleated	squeaked	replied	said

Saying verbs for people	Saying verbs for animals
asked	buzzed

Let's have fun!

Draw a picture to show what is happening in each of the sentences below.

I **whispered** to my friend.	"I've cut my knee," I **groaned**.
"See you later," she **called** as she jumped from the bus.	"You can't wear that to school!" we **giggled**.

Let's have a test!

In questions 1–3, which word is a saying verb?

1
- ◯ ran
- ◯ said
- ◯ helped
- ◯ tried

2
- ◯ walked
- ◯ stopped
- ◯ screamed
- ◯ rested

3
- ◯ hooted
- ◯ hopped
- ◯ swam
- ◯ cut

In questions 4–6, which saying verb goes in the space?

4 "Get out of the way quickly," ______________________ the farmer.
- ◯ mooed
- ◯ called
- ◯ quacked
- ◯ neighed

5 She ______________________ the song well.
- ◯ watched
- ◯ patted
- ◯ sent
- ◯ sang

6 He ______________________ me they were moving to the country.
- ◯ told
- ◯ asked
- ◯ suggested
- ◯ explained

In questions 7–8, which sentence contains a saying verb?

7
- ◯ "Do not come near the horse," said the vet.
- ◯ The vet looked at the sick horse.
- ◯ The horse was lame.
- ◯ The horse needs a vet.

8
- ◯ The farm animals were hungry.
- ◯ She warmed milk for the lamb.
- ◯ They bought some hay for the animals.
- ◯ We begged her to let us feed the hens.

Let's write now!

Write a **narrative** about two people or animals who have an argument. Use different **saying verbs** to express how they speak to each other.

Unit 9 Getting and giving

Focus
Simple sentences; full stops

A present for Kim

Kim looked unhappy. He had broken his arm. He couldn't ride his tricycle. He felt sad.

Julie and I went to the supermarket. We wanted to find Kim a present. We couldn't find anything for a long time. Then we saw a plastic submarine. We knew he would like it.

We counted our money. We were five cents short. We counted our money again. Hurray! We'd made a mistake. We had enough money after all.

Kim untied his parcel. He loved his submarine! He forgot to be sad.

This is another **narrative**. It is made up of **simple sentences** that tell a story about buying a present.

A **simple sentence** is a group of words that makes sense by itself. It has only one verb. It begins with a capital letter and ends with a full stop; for example, **Kim looked unhappy.**

Let's find them!

Find the **simple sentences** in the text that answer the questions.

For example: What had Kim done to his arm? He had broken his arm.

1. What couldn't Kim ride? ______________________

____

2. How did Kim feel? ______________________
3. What did Kim do with his parcel? ______________________
4. What did Kim forget? ______________________

Let's go to the next step!

Add a verb from the box to the spaces below to make a **simple sentence**. The first letter of each verb has been given to help you.

For example: We h*elped* __________ the sick boy.

bought	wrote	posted	saved	pushed	gave	helped

1. Auntie Jill g__________ me a present.
2. I b__________ a CD.
3. I s__________ my pocket money.
4. He w__________ a shopping list.
5. Mum p__________ the parcel.
6. We p__________ our shopping trolley to the check out.

Let's aim high now!

The words below are jumbled up. Re-order them so they make **simple sentences**.

For example: her Sally purse lost. *Sally lost her purse.*

1. boy He helped the. __________
2. book her I gave a. __________
3. drove Dad home. __________
4. shop The sold toys. __________
5. new has He shoes. __________
6. her a present We gave. __________

Our jumble sale

Our school had a jumble sale. We raised money for Animal Rescue.

Firstly, we looked at home for things to give. I found books and toys. Then the teachers set up stalls.

Our jumble sale opened at nine am. Lots of people came.

We had a magic show. There were free balloons. There were jugglers as well.

We counted the money from the jumble sale. We made $320 for Animal Rescue. We all felt very pleased.

by Charlie

This is another **recount**. Charlie uses **simple sentences** to tell about the jumble sale he had at his school.

Remember that a **simple sentence** is a group of words that makes sense by itself. It has only one verb. It begins with a capital letter and ends with a **full stop**; for example, **Our school had a jumble sale.**

Let's find them!

Find the **simple sentences** in the text that answer the questions.

For example:

What did Charlie's school raise money for? *We raised money for Animal Rescue.*

1. What did the children do first? ______________________

2. When did their jumble sale open? ______________________

3. How much money did they make? ______________________

4. How did they all feel? ______________________

Let's go to the next step!

Complete these **simple sentences** by choosing a verb from the box. The first one has been done for you.

shared	counted	posted	lent	gave	went	won

1. She ___lent___ me a new book.
2. She ______________ a prize.
3. I ______________ her a get-well card.
4. She ______________ me a drink of water.
5. She ______________ her fruit with me.
6. I ______________ to the shops.
7. We ______________ the money.

Let's aim high now!

Circle the verbs in these **simple sentences**.
For example: We (made) $320 for Animal Rescue.

1. The juggler hurt his foot.
2. We watched the magic show.
3. She bought six peaches.
4. I ate some banana cake.
5. Animal Rescue helps animals.
6. I liked the jugglers.

Let's put it together now!

Count how many **simple sentences** there are in this story. Write the number below.

Dad drove me to the shops. He parked the car. We bought some shopping. We pushed our trolley to the car park. Our car was gone!

Then I remembered something. We had parked on the green level. We were on the pink level. Dad turned pink as well!

There are ______________________ **simple sentences** in this story.

Let's have fun!

Match the **simple sentences** to the pictures by drawing a line to connect them. The first one has been done for you.

- Sal put a bandaid on her knee.
- Scott took the dog for a walk.
- I painted a poster.
- Dad looked for his car.
- He bandaged the dog's paw.

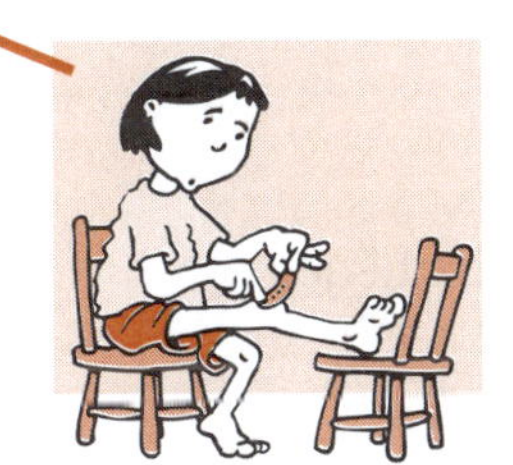

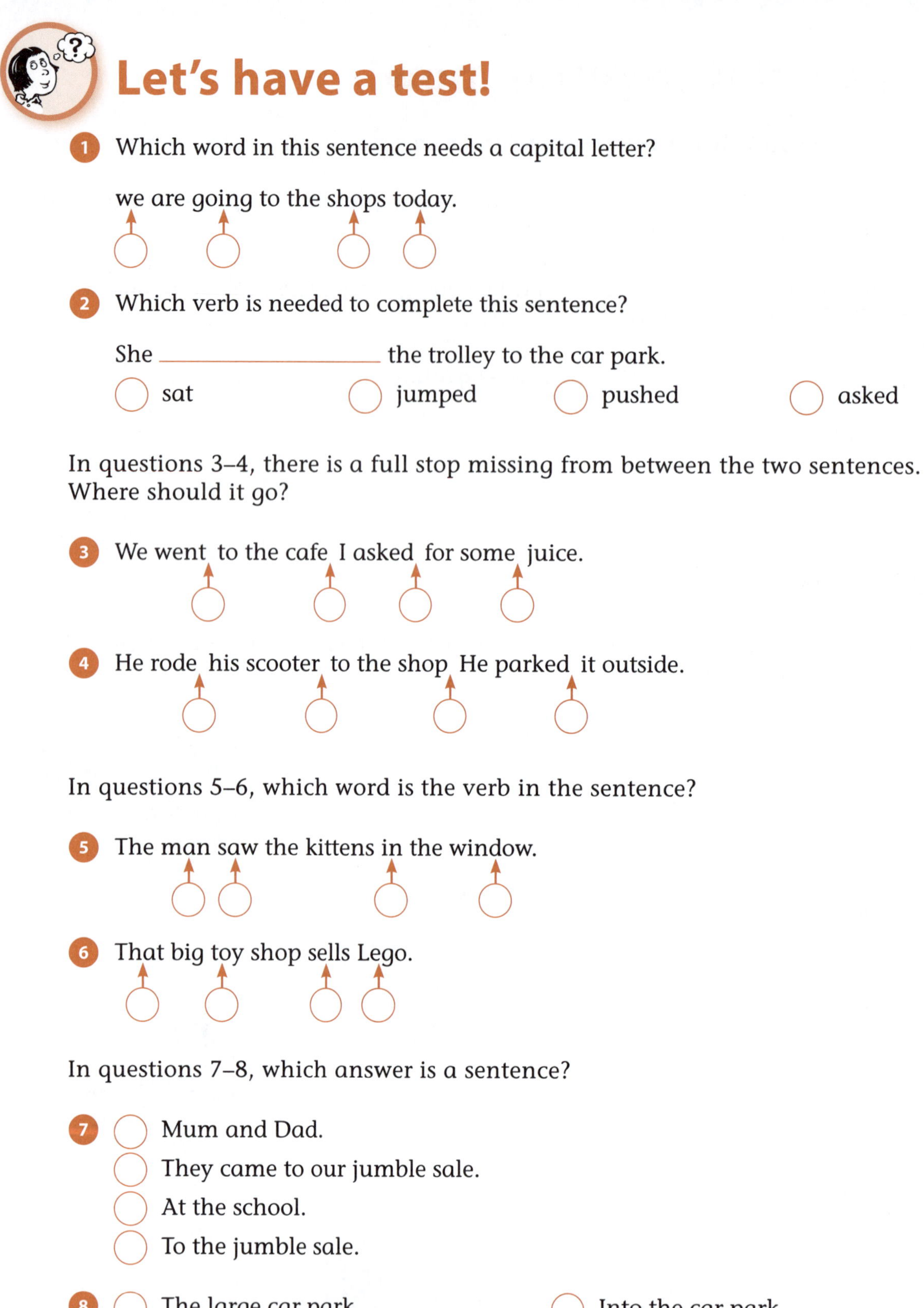

Let's have a test!

1. Which word in this sentence needs a capital letter?

   we are going to the shops today.

2. Which verb is needed to complete this sentence?

   She ______________ the trolley to the car park.

   ◯ sat ◯ jumped ◯ pushed ◯ asked

In questions 3–4, there is a full stop missing from between the two sentences. Where should it go?

3. We went to the cafe I asked for some juice.

4. He rode his scooter to the shop He parked it outside.

In questions 5–6, which word is the verb in the sentence?

5. The man saw the kittens in the window.

6. That big toy shop sells Lego.

In questions 7–8, which answer is a sentence?

7. ◯ Mum and Dad.
   ◯ They came to our jumble sale.
   ◯ At the school.
   ◯ To the jumble sale.

8. ◯ The large car park.
   ◯ In the car.
   ◯ Into the car park.
   ◯ She drove home.

Let's write now!

Write a **narrative** about a lost dog. Use **simple sentences** to tell your story.

Unit 10 Doing things differently

Focus
More simple sentences

Flags

My class made a flag display. It showed flags from lots of different countries. I made a flag for Vietnam. I painted it red. Then I pasted a yellow star on it. My grandparents came here from Vietnam.

Angelo made a Greek flag. His parents came from Greece. He painted white stripes with blue in between. He placed a cross in the top corner.

Our teacher made an Australian flag. Tommy painted it red, white and blue. I stuck stars on it. Kathy painted a black, red and yellow Aboriginal flag. Its yellow circle looked like a sun.

by Tuyen

This is a **recount**. Tuyen uses **simple sentences** to tell who and what do things in her recount about the flag display.

Simple sentences tell who or what does the action. You find out by asking who or what about the verb; for example, Who or what made a flag display? **My class**.

Let's find them!

Find who or what in the text did the actions in these **simple sentences**.
For example: Who made a flag for Vietnam? I (Tuyen)

1. Who came here from Vietnam? ______________________
2. Who made a Greek flag? ______________________
3. Who made an Australian flag? ______________________
4. Who painted an Aboriginal flag? ______________________

Let's go to the next step!

Who or what is doing the action in these **simple sentences**?

For example: Chickens go 'gut gut' in Turkey. Chickens

1 Birds go 'cui cui' in France. ______

2 Dogs go 'waf waf' in Holland. ______

3 Bees go 'bzz bzz' in England. ______

4 Lions go 'rrr rrr' in Russia. ______

5 Cats go 'nyaa nyaa' in Japan. ______

6 Pigs go 'grunz' In Germany. ______

Let's aim high now!

The word order is wrong in these **simple sentences**. Change the word order so the right common noun is doing the action.

For example: The corn pecked the chicken. The chicken pecked the corn.

1 The dog food gulped the dog. ______

2 The straw chewed the goat. ______

3 The cow milked the man. ______

4 The grass nibbled the rabbit. ______

5 The milk drank the cat. ______

Fun at the food fair

Ben and Huong went to the food fair together. They saw food from different countries on the stalls.

Ben bought dim sum and pizza. Huong bought sushi and fruit salad. Just then Timmy, the dog, rushed past. Timmy was chasing a cat. Timmy knocked Ben over. **Ben dropped his food on the ground**. His eyes filled with tears.

The owner of the dim sum stall gave them more dim sum. Ben and Huong ate their food with smiles on their faces.

This is another **narrative**. It uses **simple sentences** to tell who and what do things at the food fair.

Remember that **simple sentences** tell who or what is doing the action; for example, **<u>Ben</u> dropped his food on the ground**.

Let's find them!

Find who or what in the text did the actions in these **simple sentences**.

For example: Who went to the food fair together? Ben and Huong

1. Who bought dim sum and pizza? ______
2. Who bought sushi and fruit salad? ______
3. Who was chasing a cat? ______
4. Who dropped his food? ______
5. Who gave them free dim sum? ______

Let's go to the next step!

Underline the words that tell who or what does the action in these **simple sentences**.
For example: Maggie often plays Snakes and Ladders.

1. This kite flies very high.
2. My brother lost my dice.
3. We played hopscotch for hours.
4. Suri loves to skip.
5. Stories keep you interested.
6. Bill and I like board games.

Let's aim high now!

Underline the verbs in these **simple sentences**. Then circle the words that tell who or what does the actions.
For example: (They) ate curry and rice.

1. She made some noodles.
2. I bought a doner kebab.
3. We had yum cha today.
4. The cook made a stir-fry.
5. They bought some fruit salad.
6. Dad cooked us spaghetti.

Let's put it together now!

Sue has left out full stops and capital letters from her **simple sentences** in this story. Add them in the right places.

> **Tip!**
> There are seven verbs and seven **simple sentences**.

Cats and dogs

my dog chased a cat the cat ran up a tree it was stuck in the tree mum found a ladder she helped the cat down safely our dog was in trouble he was put in the dog house!

Let's have fun!

Who is doing the action in these **simple sentences**? The pictures will help you complete them.

1. The _ _ _ is eating an apple.
2. The _ _ _ _ is eating some noodles.
3. The _ _ _ is barking at the cat.
4. The _ _ _ is running up the tree.

Think of your own **simple sentence**.
Draw a picture that shows who is doing the action in your sentence. Write your sentence under the picture.

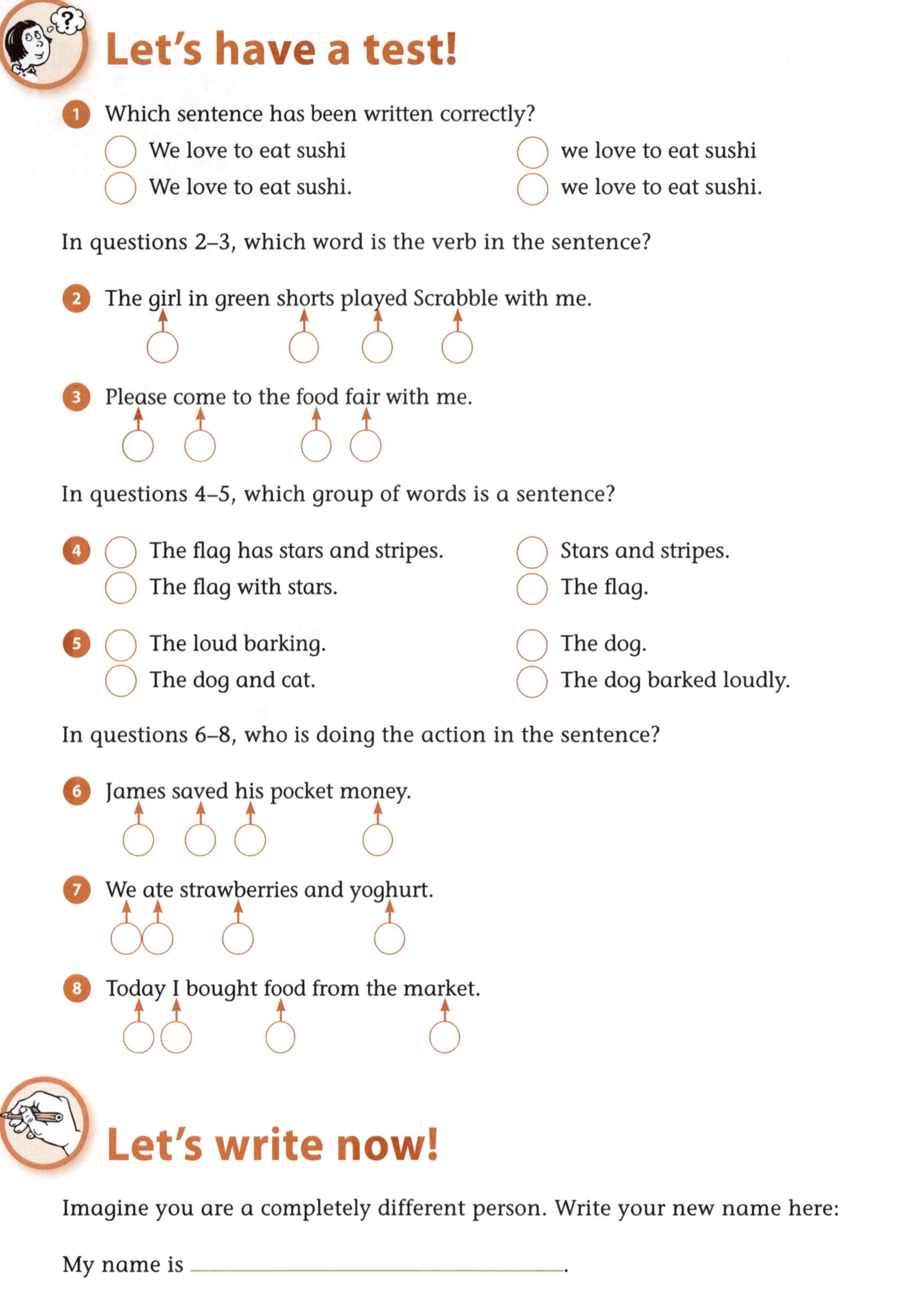

Let's have a test!

1. Which sentence has been written correctly?
   - ◯ We love to eat sushi
   - ◯ We love to eat sushi.
   - ◯ we love to eat sushi
   - ◯ we love to eat sushi.

In questions 2–3, which word is the verb in the sentence?

2. The girl in green shorts played Scrabble with me.
   (◯ girl ◯ shorts ◯ played ◯ Scrabble)

3. Please come to the food fair with me.
   (◯ Please ◯ come ◯ food ◯ fair)

In questions 4–5, which group of words is a sentence?

4. - ◯ The flag has stars and stripes.
   - ◯ The flag with stars.
   - ◯ Stars and stripes.
   - ◯ The flag.

5. - ◯ The loud barking.
   - ◯ The dog and cat.
   - ◯ The dog.
   - ◯ The dog barked loudly.

In questions 6–8, who is doing the action in the sentence?

6. James saved his pocket money.
   (◯ James ◯ saved ◯ his ◯ money)

7. We ate strawberries and yoghurt.
   (◯ We ◯ ate ◯ strawberries ◯ yoghurt)

8. Today I bought food from the market.
   (◯ Today ◯ I ◯ food ◯ market)

Let's write now!

Imagine you are a completely different person. Write your new name here:

My name is ________________________________.

Now write a **recount** about how you spent a special day in 'your' life. Use **simple sentences** to tell what happened.

Unit 11 Telling stories

Adverbs

Tiddalik

Tiddalik jumped **boldly** onto his lily pad. **Thirstily** he drank the water from his pond. Then he greedily swallowed the water in the rivers. He slowly filled his body with all the water in the land. There was no water left for the other animals.

The animals secretly planned to trick him. They'd make him laugh so the water could escape. They did funny dances before him. Tiddalik didn't even smile.

The eel was angry with Tiddalik. He spoke crossly to him. He twisted about like a corkscrew. Tiddalik laughed loudly! The water poured quickly from his mouth. Soon the waterholes were full again.

This is another **narrative**. It uses adverbs to tell how characters do things in the Dreamtime story.

Adverbs are words that add meaning to verbs. They can tell how things are done; for example, (jumped) **boldly**, (drank) **thirstily**.

Let's find them!

Find the **adverb** in the text that tells how about the verb.

For example: swallowed ___greedily___

1. filled ________________
2. planned ________________
3. spoke ________________
4. laughed ________________
5. poured ________________

Tip!

Adverbs often end in **ly**. Some examples are **quickly**, **slowly**, **bravely**, **secretly**, **swiftly**, **kindly**, **happily** and **quietly**.

Let's go to the next step!

Underline the **adverb** that tells how about the verb in these sentences.
For example: Tiddalik drank thirstily.

1. Tiddalik drank greedily.
2. The animals planned secretly.
3. The eel spoke crossly.
4. Tiddalik laughed loudly.
5. The water flowed swiftly.
6. The drought ended quickly.

Let's aim high now!

Choose an **adverb** from the box that tells how about the verb. The first letter is given to help you.
For example: The mother kangaroo acted k<u>indly</u>________.

quickly	snugly	gladly	kindly	gently	bravely

1. The kangaroo patted the old wombat g________________.
2. The kangaroo b________________ chased the hunter.
3. The wombat q________________ turned into a spirit.
4. The spirit g________________ gave the kangaroo a pouch.
5. The joey fitted s________________ into her new pouch.

The Rainbow Serpent

The Rainbow Serpent moved **slowly** across the land. He looked **eagerly** for his tribe. As he went, his heavy body made rivers and mountains in the earth. Finally, he found his tribe.

Two boys bravely asked the Serpent for shelter. But the Serpent rudely ate the boys! His tribe shouted angrily. Swiftly they cut the boys from the Serpent's tummy. The boys turned into birds. Then the tribe chased away the Rainbow Serpent.

The Serpent slid quickly into the sea. Sometimes you can see him shining in the sky.

This is another **narrative**. It uses adverbs to tell how things are done.

Remember that **adverbs** are words that add meaning to verbs. They can tell how things are done; for example, (moved) **slowly**, (looked) **eagerly**.

Let's find them!

Find the **adverb** that tells how about the verb. The first one has been done for you.

1. found finally
2. asked ____________
3. ate ____________
4. shouted ____________
5. cut ____________
6. slid ____________

Let's go to the next step!

Choose an **adverb** from the box that tells how about the verb. The first letter has been given to help you.

For example: The children listened e agerly .

quickly	eagerly	correctly	loudly	brightly	angrily

1. The teacher spoke l____________________.
2. They answered the questions c____________________.
3. The animals shouted a____________________.
4. The birds flew away q____________________.
5. The rainbow shone b____________________ in the sky.

Let's aim high now!

Underline the **adverb** that tells how in these sentences.

For example: We cheerfully sang a song about the Rainbow Serpent.

1. The teacher carefully hung our wet paintings to dry.
2. "Hold each other's waists," she said firmly.
3. We easily made a long serpent with our bodies.
4. We glided smoothly around the room together.
5. I moved slowly like a serpent.
6. The children cheered loudly at the end of the lesson.

Let's put it together now!

There are five **adverbs** that have lost their *ly* tails in this story. Find them and rewrite them correctly on the lines below.

The farmer and the rabbit

The farmer crept quiet towards the rabbit. The rabbit pricked up his ears. Footsteps were coming slow towards him. His burrow was nearby. He'd hop there as quick as he could. Would he get there in time?

The farmer saw the rabbit move. He ran swift towards him. He was too late. The rabbit had made it safe home.

1. ______________________
2. ______________________
3. ______________________
4. ______________________
5. ______________________

Let's have fun!

Join the sentences to the pictures they describe. Underline the **adverbs**. The first one has been done for you.

- The frog drank thirstily.
- The eel frowned angrily.
- The kookaburras laughed happily.
- The emus danced crazily.
- The kangaroo nodded wisely.
- The rain fell heavily.

Let's have a test!

In questions 1–4, which word tells how about the verb in each sentence?

1. The kangaroo kindly helped the old wombat.
2. The teacher told the story clearly.
3. The Rainbow Serpent moved slowly across the land.
4. I easily remembered the story of Tiddalik.
5. Which sentence tells how the eel spoke?
   - The eel spoke after the frog.
   - The eel spoke angrily.
   - The eel spoke later.
   - The eel spoke in front of the frog.
6. Which sentence tells how Tiddalik laughed?
   - Tiddalik laughed loudly.
   - Tiddalik laughed at the eel.
   - Tiddalik laughed afterwards.
   - Tiddalik laughed.
7. Which sentence tells how the children listened?
   - The children listened.
   - The children listened to the story.
   - The children listened to the teacher.
   - The children listened quietly.
8. Which sentence tells how the kangaroo chased the hunter?
   - The kangaroo bravely chased the hunter.
   - The hunter chased the kangaroo into the bush.
   - The kangaroo chased the hunter.
   - The hunter chased the kangaroo.

Let's write now!

Make up a **narrative** about an animal. Firstly, tell someone in your family what happens in your story. Then write your story down. Use **adverbs** to make the action lively.

Unit 12 Celebrating

Phrases

The street party

On Saturday, our street held a street party. We had a picnic **in the park**. We were celebrating the New Year. Everyone took plates of food to the park. We sat on chairs and rugs. Then we shared all the yummy food.

Our family brought pizza. Our neighbours, the Chens, put doner kebabs on their plate. Doner kebabs are a Turkish food.

We had lemonade after lunch. I was thirsty and drank mine all at once.

We played games in the afternoon. I liked playing with the frisbee the best.

by Hiroko

This is another **recount**. Hiroko uses **phrases** to add information about when and where things happen at the street party.

Phrases are groups of words that add information to sentences. They do not have a verb. They can tell where and when; for example, **On Saturday** (when) **in the park** (where).

Let's find them!

Find the **phrase** in the text that answers these questions.

For example: Where did everyone take their plates of food? *to the park*

1. Where did people sit? ______________________
2. Where did the Chens put doner kebabs? ______________________
3. When did they have lemonade? ______________________
4. When did Hiroko drink her lemonade? ______________________
5. When did they play games? ______________________

Let's go to the next step!

Underline the **phrase** that tells where in these sentences.
For example: They played games <u>at her party</u>.

1. She baked the birthday cake in the kitchen.
2. I bought her birthday present at the market.
3. Her party was held at the zoo.
4. She blew up the balloons outside the tent.
5. We put the strawberries on paper plates.
6. They went to the wedding.

Let's aim high now!

Underline the **phrase** in the text that tells when in these sentences.
For example: We had the celebration <u>in the afternoon</u>.

1. The team practised before school.
2. The Book Fair is after the holidays.
3. They sang happy birthday after lunch.
4. We celebrated Chinese New Year after sunset.
5. Our term ends in two days.
6. My party will be on September 1st.

Lily's Diary

2nd June

Dear Diary

I am staying **at Nana's and Papa's house**. Their 50th wedding anniversary is **in two days**. They are having a big party at their house! It will be held in the afternoon.

I love Nana and Papa. They are never mean to anyone.

A van arrived at nine o'clock. There was a big box in the back. A man carried the box into the kitchen. There was a cake inside the box. Mum hid the box in the cupboard. I peeped into the box. The cake looked beautiful.

I can't wait for the party.

by Lily

This is a **diary entry**. Remember that diary entries are daily events written about in a diary. Lily uses **phrases** to tell where and when things happen at her grandparents' house.

Remember that **phrases** are groups of words that do not have a verb. They can tell where and when; for example, **at Nana's and Papa's house** (where), **in two days** (when).

Let's find them!

Find the **phrase** in the text that answers these questions.

For example: Where were they having a big party? *at their house*

1. When will the party be held? __________
2. When did the van arrive? __________
3. Where was the big box? __________
4. Where was the cake? __________
5. Where did Mum hide the box? __________
6. Where did Lily peep? __________

Let's go to the next step!

Circle the **phrases** in these sentences that tell when about the verb.
For example: They made her cake after breakfast.

1. She blew up the balloons before the party.

2. The party began at two o'clock.

Circle the **phrases** in these sentences that tell where about the verb.
For example: Her party was held at the zoo.

3. The party was at her house.

4. We put the fruit on the plates.

5. I hid her present in the attic.

Let's aim high now!

Do the underlined **phrases** tell when or where about the verbs in these sentences?
For example: Dad **sang** happy birthday on the porch. where

1. They **found** their presents after lunch. ____________________

2. They **celebrated** at the street party. ____________________

3. She **iced** their cake before breakfast. ____________________

4. The fireworks **shone** brightly in the dark. ____________________

5. The balloon **floated** past the tree. ____________________

6. The party **ended** by 8 o'clock. ____________________

Let's put it together now!

Match the sentence below to its picture. Use the **phrases** to help you choose the correct sentence.

1

2

3

4
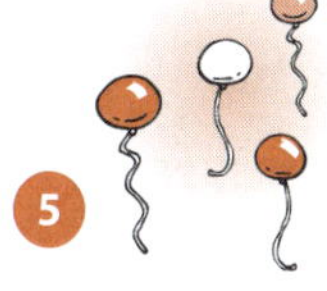
5

6

- The present is on the tree in picture number ____________________.
- The balloons are floating in the sky in picture number ____________________.
- The presents are under the tree in picture number ____________________.
- The cake is on the table in picture number ____________________.
- The cake is next to the glasses in picture number ____________________.
- The balloons are tied to the pole in picture number ____________________.

Let's have fun!

Draw these things on the picture below.

- a rainbow across the sky
- food on the rug
- children on the grass
- a frisbee in the air
- a chair under the tree
- a person in the chair

Let's have a test!

In questions 1–2, which is the phrase in the sentence?

1. The birthday party was held at our house.
   - ◯ The birthday party was held
   - ◯ The birthday party
   - ◯ at our house
   - ◯ was held at our house

2. They celebrated the New Year by the water.
   - ◯ They celebrated the New Year
   - ◯ They celebrated
   - ◯ the New Year
   - ◯ by the water

In questions 3–5, which answer has a phrase?

3.
   - ◯ The picnic was fun.
   - ◯ The picnic went well.
   - ◯ The picnic was in the park.
   - ◯ The picnic was over.

4.
   - ◯ We played hide-and-seek.
   - ◯ We played hide-and-seek near the house.
   - ◯ We played hide-and-seek here.
   - ◯ We played hide-and seek noisily.

5.
   - ◯ We had our picnic on the picnic rug.
   - ◯ We had our picnic.
   - ◯ We had our picnic today.
   - ◯ We had our picnic yesterday.

6. Which sentence does **not** have a phrase?
   - ◯ The moon shone brightly in the sky.
   - ◯ The moon shone brightly.
   - ◯ The moon shone in the evening.
   - ◯ The moon shone brightly on Friday night.

7. Which sentence has a phrase that tells when?
   - ◯ He blew up the balloons after breakfast.
   - ◯ He blew up the balloons at my place.
   - ◯ He blew up the balloons at his place.
   - ◯ He blew up the balloons in the kitchen.

8. Which sentence has a phrase that tells where?
   - ◯ I went to the fête on Saturday.
   - ◯ I went to the fête in the afternoon.
   - ◯ I went to the fête at 9 o'clock.
   - ◯ I went to the fête across the road.

Let's write now!

Write a **recount** of being at a birthday party. Use **phrases** to tell where and when things happened at the party.

Unit 13 Talking about time

Focus
Questions and statements; question marks; full stops

About time!

"Is it time to go to school, Mum?"

"I told you a minute ago, Billy. Not yet. Don't you remember?"

Later ...

"Is it time to go home yet, Ms Kidd?"

"I told you a minute ago, Billy. Not yet. Don't you remember?"

Later ...

"Is this present for me, Auntie Jean?"

"Yes, Billy. Now you can learn to tell the time."

"Wow! A watch. Thank you! Will you teach me, please Dad?"

"Of course, Billy. Are you ready?"

These are **conversations**. Conversations are spoken exchanges between people. Billy uses **questions** to ask for information about the time.

Questions are sentences that ask for information. They always end with a **question mark** (**?**); for example, "**Is it time to go to school, Mum?**"

Let's find them!

Find the **questions** in the text.

For example: Billy asks his teacher "Is it time to go home yet, Ms Kidd?"

1. Billy's teacher asks him ______________________________

2. Billy asks his Auntie Jean ______________________________

____

3. Billy asks his father ______________________________

4. Billy's father asks Billy ______________________________

Let's go to the next step!

These sentences have lost their final punctuation marks. Give them a **full stop** or a **question mark** to make them complete. The first one has been done for you.

1. Will you be ready in time ?
2. I was ready in time
3. What time will the bell ring
4. Are you coming over this afternoon
5. She came over to my house
6. When are you leaving
7. The plane leaves shortly

Let's aim high now!

Some of the sentences below are **questions** and some are not. Write *question* or *not a question* beside each.

For example: Are you coming to school today? question

1. Is your watch mended now? __________
2. How long does it take? __________
3. I'll be late for the game. __________
4. When is your birthday? __________
5. My friend is coming over tomorrow. __________
6. Did it happen a long time ago? __________

Pip's interview

"How did people tell the time in the past, Grandpa?"

"They used the sun, moon and stars, Pip."

"What else did they do?"

"They made sundials."

"What's a sundial, Grandpa?"

"A sundial tells the time."

"How does that work?"

"A shadow falls on its face."

"Is it like a clock face?"

"Yes, it has hours marked on its face.

Would you like a watch, Pip?"

"Yes, I'd like a digital watch, Grandpa."

This is another **conversation**. Pip asks **questions** about how people used to tell the time. His grandfather replies with **statements**, which are sentences that give information.

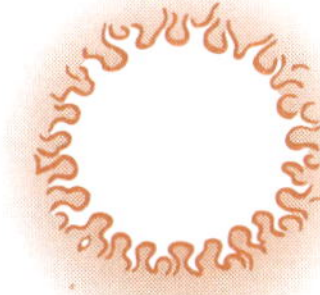

Statements are sentences that give information. They always end with a **full stop**; for example, **They used the sun, moon and stars, Pip.**

Let's find them!

Find the **statements** in the conversation that answer these **questions**.

For example: "What else did they do?" "They made sundials."

1. "What's a sundial, Grandpa?" ______
2. "How does that work?" ______
3. "Is it like a clock face?" ______
4. "Would you like a watch, Pip?" ______

Let's go to the next step!

Where does the **full stop** go to separate these **statements** and **questions**? For example: I am six. How old are you?

1. She is seven How old is your sister?

3. He isn't hungry now Why is he crying?

4. We don't have a sundial in our garden Do you?

5. We have always lived here Where do you live?

6. My grandpa has a pocket watch Does yours?

7. I saw a water clock on TV Have you seen one?

Let's aim high now!

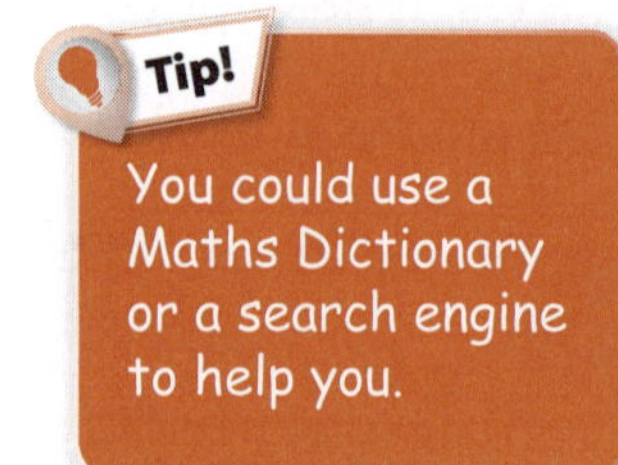

Number the **statement** with the number of the question it matches. The first one has been done for you.

Questions	Statements
1 How many seconds are there in a minute?	1 There are 60 seconds in a minute.
2 How many minutes are there in an hour?	____ There are 12 months in a year.
3 How many hours are there in a day?	____ There are seven days in a week.
4 How many days are there in a week?	____ There are 52 weeks in a year.
5 How many weeks are there in a year?	____ There are four seasons in a year.
6 How many months are there in a year?	____ There are 60 minutes in an hour.
7 How many seasons are there in a year?	____ There are 24 hours in a day.

Let's put it together now!

Fill in the missing word from each **question** to solve the crossword.

Questions often begin with words such as **How**, **What**, **When**, **Which**, **Who**, **Where**, **Will**, **Why**, **Are** and **Did**.

1				2						3		
4		5										
6												

ACROSS

2. ____________ day is your birthday?
3. ____________ is coming to your party?
4. ____________ long until lunchtime?
6. ____________ you able to tell the time?

DOWN

1. ____________ did the bell ring?
2. ____________ is the time now?
3. ____________ you arrive in ten minutes?
5. ____________ did you put my watch?

Let's have fun!

Choose a topic you would like to learn more about. Think of three **questions** to ask about your topic. Find out the answers to your questions.

My topic is ____.

My **questions** are:

1. ____
2. ____
3. ____

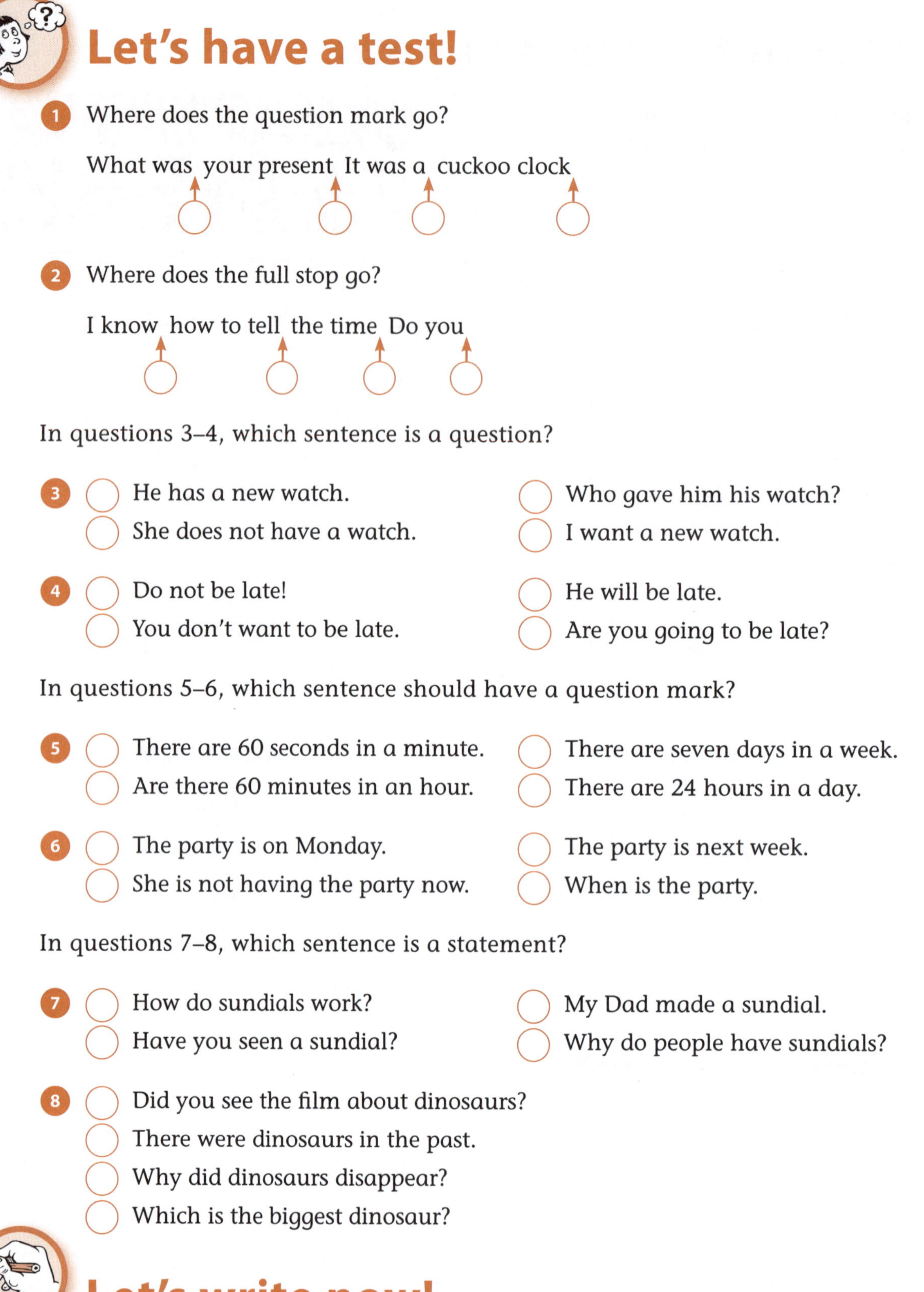

Let's have a test!

1. Where does the question mark go?

   What was your present It was a cuckoo clock

2. Where does the full stop go?

   I know how to tell the time Do you

In questions 3–4, which sentence is a question?

3. ◯ He has a new watch.
   ◯ She does not have a watch.
   ◯ Who gave him his watch?
   ◯ I want a new watch.

4. ◯ Do not be late!
   ◯ You don't want to be late.
   ◯ He will be late.
   ◯ Are you going to be late?

In questions 5–6, which sentence should have a question mark?

5. ◯ There are 60 seconds in a minute.
   ◯ Are there 60 minutes in an hour.
   ◯ There are seven days in a week.
   ◯ There are 24 hours in a day.

6. ◯ The party is on Monday.
   ◯ She is not having the party now.
   ◯ The party is next week.
   ◯ When is the party.

In questions 7–8, which sentence is a statement?

7. ◯ How do sundials work?
   ◯ Have you seen a sundial?
   ◯ My Dad made a sundial.
   ◯ Why do people have sundials?

8. ◯ Did you see the film about dinosaurs?
   ◯ There were dinosaurs in the past.
   ◯ Why did dinosaurs disappear?
   ◯ Which is the biggest dinosaur?

Let's write now!

Write a **conversation** between two people. Include at least two **questions** and two **statements**.

Unit 14 Taking care

Focus

Statements, commands and requests

This is **a set of rules**. Rules tell us how to behave. They list **commands** to follow in the home to help the environment.

Caring for the environment

Our family has a set of rules.

- **Save water.**
- Turn the TV off when not watching.
- Switch off unused lights.
- Recycle plastic, glass and paper.
- Put scraps in the compost.
- Take short showers.
- Never waste paper.

Commands are sentences that tell (or order) someone to do something; for example, **Save water.**

Let's find them!

Find the verbs in the **commands** that tell what must be done (or not done) in the rules. The first one has been done for you.

1. Turn
2. ____________________
3. ____________________
4. ____________________
5. ____________________
6. ____________________

Let's go to the next step!

Are these sentences **commands** or **statements**?
Write your answer on the lines.

For example:
Our bottles are in the bin. statement

Tip!
Remember: **statements** are sentences that give information.

1. Put your bottles in the recycle bin. ____________________
2. Don't waste paper. ____________________
3. Recycling paper saves cutting down trees. ____________________
4. Get a worm farm today. ____________________
5. Worm farms recycle waste. ____________________
6. Put those scraps in the compost. ____________________

Let's aim high now!

Number the **command** with the number of the **statement** that it matches. The first one has been done for you.

Statement	Command
1 He recycled his drink cans.	____ Don't use plastic bags.
2 She put her litter in the bin.	____ Walk to work to save fuel.
3 He recycled his mobile phone.	____ Put litter in the bin.
4 He uses a worm farm to recycle waste.	1 Recycle your drink cans.
5 We don't use plastic bags.	____ Use a rainwater tank.
6 She walks to work to save fuel.	____ Recycle your mobile phone.
7 They use a rainwater tank.	____ Use a worm farm to recycle waste.

Caring for each other

Dear Olly and James,
We will be home about 10:30. Your babysitter tonight is Aunt Harriet.
Don't forget to clean your teeth. Be in bed by 8 pm. **Olly, would you phone Gran, please?** She wants you to explain something to her. James, would you put the bin out for us? Would you feed the cat too, please?
Your teacher sent us an email about your visit to the zoo. You must return the forms tomorrow. Pack them into your bags tonight. That way you won't forget.
Last request. Will you look take good care of Aunt Harriet?
Love
Mum and Dad xxxx

This is another **letter**. Mum and Dad give **commands** and make **requests** to Olly and James in a letter left for them.

Requests are questions that politely ask people to do something; for example, **Olly, would you phone Gran, please?**

Let's find them!

Find four **commands** and three **requests** in the text. The first ones have been done for you.

Commands

1. Don't forget to clean your teeth.
2. ______________________
3. ______________________
   ____
4. ______________________

Requests

5. James, would you put the bin out for us?
6. ______________________
7. ______________________
   ____

Let's go to the next step!

Are these **requests** or **commands**? Write your answer on the lines.
For example: Would you write on Tom's get-well card? ______request______

1. Would you find a seat for Mr Brown, please? ____________________
2. Always give your seat to an older person. ____________________
3. Will you carry Gran's parcels, please? ____________________
4. May I have a turn, please? ____________________
5. Always say please and thank you. ____________________
6. May I have some sunscreen for my nose, please? ____________________

Let's aim high now!

Number the **request** with the number of the **command** that it matches. The first one has been done for you.

Command	Request
1 Eat your vegetables.	____ Will you keep off the grass, please?
2 Take out the rubbish.	____ Will you watch out for traffic, please?
3 Clean up that mess.	____ Will you pass me the sauce, please?
4 Don't walk on the grass.	____ Will you clean up that mess, please?
5 Clean your teeth.	____ Will you take out the rubbish, please?
6 Watch out for traffic.	____ Will you clean your teeth, please?
7 Pass the sauce.	__1__ Will you eat your vegetables, please?

Let's put it together now!

Sam saves stickers. He pastes them on his suitcase. Some of the letters have rubbed off. Can you fill in the missing letters?

KEEP OFF THE G ___ ___ ___ ___

SAVE THE WH ___ ___ ___ S

KEEP AUS ___ ___ ___ ___ ___ A BEAUTI ___ ___ ___

BEWARE OF THE ___ ___ ___

SAVE OUR P ___ ___ ___ ___T

WA ___ ___ ___ OUT F ___ ___ CYCL ___ ___ ___ ___

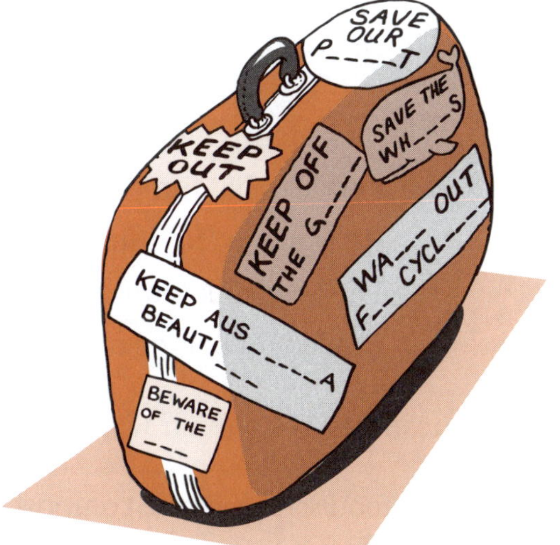

Let's have fun!

Play the game *Annie Asks* with friends or family members. It is like *Simon Says* but **requests** are made instead of **commands**.

The person who is Annie makes **requests** such as:

Annie asks if you'll stand on one leg.

Annie asks if you'll put your elbow on your ear.

Annie asks if you'll jump in the air.

Then suddenly Annie makes a **command** such as:

Sit on the floor.

Pinch your big toes.

Reach for the sky.

When Annie gives a **command** instead of a **request** anyone who moves to obey is out of the game.

Let's have a test!

1. Which sentence is a statement?
   - ◯ Keep your room tidy.
   - ◯ His room was always tidy.
   - ◯ Would you tidy your room now?
   - ◯ You must tidy your room.

2. Which sentence needs a question mark?
   - ◯ I have a 'No Junk Mail' sticker.
   - ◯ He wants a 'No Junk Mail' sticker.
   - ◯ The 'No Junk Mail' stickers are all sold.
   - ◯ Could you get me a 'No Junk Mail' sticker.

In questions 3–4, which word is the verb in the command?

3. Put food scraps in the compost.

4. Save our marine mammals.

In questions 5–6, which sentence is a command?

5.
   - ◯ Plastic bags can be recycled.
   - ◯ Would you mind recycling those?
   - ◯ Recycle your plastic bags.
   - ◯ Do you recycle plastic bags?

6.
   - ◯ It is not safe to enter.
   - ◯ Do not enter.
   - ◯ Will you stay out of there, please?
   - ◯ I would rather you stayed out of there.

In questions 7–8, which sentence is a request?

7.
   - ◯ We recycle our paper.
   - ◯ Always recycle your paper.
   - ◯ Paper should be recycled.
   - ◯ Will you please recycle your paper?

8.
   - ◯ Give up your seat at once.
   - ◯ The girl gave up her seat.
   - ◯ Would you give up your seat, please?
   - ◯ Do I need to give up my seat?

Let's write now!

Make a list of five **rules** you think people should obey either at home or at school. Write them as **commands.**

Glossary of terms

Adjectives describe nouns. They give different kinds of information about the nouns they describe, e.g. six, large, red, outdoor, beautiful.

Adverbs add meaning to verbs. They tell how something happens, e.g. quickly, slowly, loudly.

Commands are sentences that tell (or order) someone to do something.

Conversations are spoken exchanges between people. They can be spoken aloud or they can be written down to report what was said.

Descriptions help us to form pictures in our mind of people, places and things.

Diary entries are daily events written about in a diary. They are written in date order.

Emails are electronic messages.

Exclamations are sentences that express strong feelings such as pleasure, surprise, anger and disgust. They end with an exclamation mark (!).

Full stops are punctuation marks placed at the end of a sentence to show it is complete. They are shown by a dot (.).

Information reports give factual information about things, e.g. mammals.

Instructions tell you how to do something.

Letters are messages in writing sent to a person.

Narratives tell a story.

Nouns are naming words. They can be singular (e.g. boy, girl) or plural (e.g. boys, girls.)

- **Common nouns** name general people, animals, places and things, e.g. girl, dog, river, ruler.
- **Proper nouns** name particular people, animals, places and things. They begin with a capital letter, e.g. Mr Scott, Lassie, Sydney, Vegemite.

Personal pronouns are words that are used in the place of nouns. They can be singular or plural, e.g. I, we.

Phrases are groups of words that do not have a verb. They can tell when and where, e.g. in the afternoon, at the museum.

Questions are sentences that ask for information. They always end with a question mark (?).

Recounts tell about events that have happened.

Requests are questions that ask someone to do something in a polite way.

Sentences are groups of words that make sense on their own. They always have a verb. They start with a capital letter and end with either a full stop, question mark or exclamation mark.

- **Simple sentences** have only one verb.

Statements are sentences that give information.

Verbs are words that show what people, animals or things do. Types of verbs are:

- **doing verbs**, e.g. jump, run
- **saying verbs**, e.g. said, shouted.

Answers

Unit 1 Beginnings

Let's find them! page 1
1 desk 2 computer 3 mouse 4 beanbags 5 books

Let's go to the next step! page 2
1 computer 2 whiteboard 3 beanbag 4 window 5 pencil

Let's aim high now! page 2
1 whiteboard 2 wall 3 poster 4 bags 5 floor

Let's find them! page 3
2 koalas 3 wombat 4 guide 5 platypus 6 animals

Let's go to the next step! page 4
1 possum 2 Bats 3 Bilbies 4 Pythons 5 lizard 6 snake

Let's aim high now! page 4
1 zookeeper 2 parents 3 friend 4 visitors 5 teacher 6 vet

Let's put it together now! page 5

Things	People	Animals
gate	vet	kangaroos
tree	driver	lizards
ticket	caretaker	wombats
cage	teacher	bilbies

Let's have fun! page 5

Let's have a test! page 6
1 snake 2 teacher 3 desk 4 leaves 5 vet 6 worker, cleaner, trainer 7 table, chair, ruler 8 rabbit

Unit 2 Holidays

Let's find them! page 7
1 park 2 town 3 backyard 4 beach

Let's go to the next step! page 8
1 garden 2 school 3 supermarket 4 oval 5 river

Let's aim high now! page 8
2 park 3 sea 4 cafe 5 postbox 6 station

Let's find them! page 9
1 swimmers 2 children 3 snorkels 4 beach 5 snake

Let's go to the next step! page 10
2 boat 3 cards 4 pilot 5 river 6 friend

Let's aim high now! page 10

Common noun	People, animals, places or things?
fruit	thing
mountains	place
kennels	place
dog	animal
friend	people
towel	thing

Let's put it together now! page 11

People	Animals	Places	Things
boy	dog	shops	postcard
child	birds	kennels	bus
woman	snake	beach	suitcase
uncle	cat	cattery	bag

Let's have fun! page 11

		1 p	o	o	l				2 m	
		l							o	
3 t	r	a	i	n					t	
		n				4 r	i	v	e	r
	5 b	e	a	6 c	h				l	
				a						
			7 t	r	a	m				

Let's have a test! page 12

1 brother, mother, father **2** hen, fox, rooster
3 toys, games, puzzles **4** river, beach, mountains
5 bus **6** guide **7** motel **8** You can't go in there because it is closed.

Unit 3 Family time

Let's find them! page 13

2 Louisa Kane **3** Bo **4** Jo **5** Popo **6** Tweet

Let's go to the next step! page 14

1 Snowball, my fluffy dog, is very cuddly.
2 Our family doctor is named Dr Knight.
3 The Wongs have moved to a new house.
4 Mr Ho is our dentist.
5 Mary wants to be a doctor.

Let's aim high now! page 14

1 She phoned **D**r **K**night.
2 Did you see our **P**rime **M**inister?
3 Our family watches **D**onald **D**uck.
4 Auntie **J**o gave me a present.
5 We will visit **U**ncle **J**ulian soon.

Let's find them! page 15

1 Desa Kiara **2** Twin Towers **3** Mandy
4 Snakes and Ladders **5** Vegemite

Let's go to the next step! page 16

1 My brother goes to the movies in Avalon.
2 Our family loves to eat at Chinatown.
3 Dad bought a Mazda that fits all the family.
4 My friend said she saw Ayers Rock.
5 We went on the Manly Ferry.

Let's aim high now! page 16

1 place **2** thing **3** place **4** thing **5** place **6** place

Let's put it together now! page 17

The **G**old **C**oast is a good place for a holiday in **A**ustralia. At **S**ea **W**orld you can see marine animals. You can see sharks swimming at **S**hark **B**ay. You can go to the **C**arrara **M**arkets. Children can have their faces painted there. There is always something to do at the **G**old **C**oast.
There were **11** missing capital letters.

Let's have a test! page 18

1 Queensland **2** Darwin **3** Spot
4 Our family went to Ayers Rock.
5 The Sydney Harbour Bridge is famous.
6 Skippy Park, Sea World, Perth
7 Sally, Tomoko, Amy **8** australia

Unit 4 Seasons

Let's find them! page 19

1 tiny, pink **2** cosy, warm **3** terrible
4 woolly, red **5** freezing, cold

Let's go to the next step! page 20

1 The rain made big puddles.
2 It was a very foggy morning.
3 He made a jolly snowman.
4 I hope we have a log fire.
5 You can expect cold weather.
6 I can see some blue sky.

Let's aim high now! page 20

1 three **2** sunny **3** black **4** cold **5** woolly
6 slippery

Let's find them! page 21

2 bare **3** freezing **4** warm **5** wobbly **6** swooping
7 scuttling **8** best

Let's go to the next step! page 22

1 Sunny **2** summer **3** outdoor **4** high
5 burning **6** wet

Let's aim high now! page 22

2 cheeky seagull
3 new swimmers
4 dead fish
5 shallow water
6 small crab

Let's put it together now! page 23

Autumn Leaves

Red leaves, brown leaves, orange leaves
Falling slowly to the hard ground
One leaf, then three, then four leaves, flutter down
They gather into deep piles in the grey gutter
Now I come and kick them about,
The crunchy leaves of autumn.

Let's have fun! page 23

1 A cheerful snowman
2 A tiny crab
3 A snowy mountain
4 A huge wave
5 A striped umbrella
6 A tall sandcastle
7 A spotted beach ball
8 A shady sunhat

Let's have a test! page 24

1 It was a cold day. 2 It was a sunny day. 3 new 4 red 5 flashing 6 large 7 woolly 8 bright

Unit 5 Animals

Let's find them! page 25

1 ears 2 beaks 3 teeth 4 brain 5 blowhole 6 water

Let's go to the next step! page 26

2 lion 3 whale 4 tiger 5 shark 6 dolphins 7 seals 8 giraffes 9 monkeys 10 animals

Let's aim high now! page 26

1 A dolphin is a playful animal.
2 Sharks have fins.
3 Penguins have flippers.
4 A dolphin is a mammal.
5 Are seals good swimmers?
6 She saw a seahorse.

Let's find them! page 27

1 zoos 2 fish 3 pictures 4 animals 5 men and women

Let's go to the next step! page 28

2 elephants 3 deer 4 birds 5 monkeys 6 men 7 children

Let's aim high now! page 28

1 singular 2 plural 3 plural 4 singular 5 plural 6 singular

Let's put it together now! page 29

We bought our tickets at the gate. We rushed into the zoo to see the animals. We saw lions prowling around. Next came the monkeys who made us laugh. We loved the giraffes. They had long necks and soft eyes. What a good day we had!

Let's have fun! page 29

c	r	b	o	q	o	z	t
l	i	o	n	s	t	o	i
s	m	e	r	f	g	o	g
u	m	p	o	h	e	s	e
m	o	n	k	e	y	s	r
s	s	o	r	e	f	t	s
g	i	r	a	f	f	e	s
h	o	s	p	a	n	z	j

Let's have a test! page 30

1 That elephant is very large.
2 The crocodile snapped his jaws.
3 Did you see any dolphins?
4 Male and female lions look different.
5 computer
6 geese
7 There are monkeyes in the zoo.
8 We watched the seales sunbake.

Unit 6 Games

Let's find them! page 31

2 He 3 We 4 I 5 I 6 him 7 I

Let's go to the next step! page 32

1 it 2 they 3 it 4 he 5 them 6 it

Let's aim high now! page 32

1 He is good at games and always wins them.
2 Did Sally tell you that she can't play today?
3 Dad said he would watch us play cricket.
4 Please keep my bat until I need it.
5 She lost some puzzle pieces but then she found them.
6 Ella chased him and then he chased her.

Let's find them! page 33

2 they 3 it 4 them 5 I 6 it

Let's go to the next step! page 34

1 He 2 I 3 me 4 They 5 We 6 you

Let's aim high now! page 34

1 them 2 we 3 She 4 he 5 him

Let's put it together now! page 35

There are **eight** personal pronouns in the text. Year One has a pod of computers that we can use. Ms Walker lets us play games on them. She chooses word games that are fun. We learn about words from them. She also lets us play adventure games where you find lost people.

Let's have fun! page 35

1 t	2 h	e	3 y		4 t		5 s	h	e
	e		o		h				
			u		e				
					6 m	e			

Let's have a test! page 36

1 I
2 we
3 They kicked three goals.
4 She likes playing card games.
5 you
6 him
7 Is Snap more fun than Fish?
8 Bill likes to play Blindman's Bluff.

Unit 7 Cooking

Let's find them! page 37

1 chop 2 rolled 3 cut 4 put 5 rubbed

Let's go to the next step! page 38

2 sprinkle 3 add 4 make 5 barbecued 6 mash 7 drink

Let's aim high now! page 38

1 slice 2 sip 3 stir 4 freeze 5 chew

Let's find them! page 39

1 Slowly add the boiling water to the jelly crystals. Stir carefully.
2 Open the can of peaches and pour 200 ml of juice and fruit into the jug. Add to the jelly mixture.
3 Place in fridge for 4 hours or more.
4 Delicious! Pat yourself on the back.

Let's go to the next step! page 40

2 went 3 ate 4 grew 5 hurried 6 learned 7 bought

Let's aim high now! page 40

1 drank William ate his spaghetti.
2 sprinkled I whipped the cream.
3 ate She washed the tablecloth.
4 chopped They drank the lemonade.
5 swallowed He patted his back.

Let's put it together now! page 41

1 c	u	2 t		3 c	o	o	k
h		a					
o		4 s	l	i	c	e	
p		t					
		5 e	a	t			

Let's have fun! page 41

1 mixed 2 cooked 3 made 4 turned 5 boiled

Let's have a test! page 42

1 cooked 2 dried 3 He ran home.
4 The dog buried his bone. 5 mixed 6 cook, eat, chop 7 Is the milk in the jug? 8 Here is your hot chocolate.

Unit 8 Life on the farm

Let's find them! page 43

2 asked 3 cried 4 shouted 5 groaned 6 agreed

Let's go to the next step! page 44

1 yelled 2 sighed 3 replied 4 called 5 asked 6 suggested

Let's aim high now! page 44

2 warned 3 grumbled 4 said 5 begged 6 whispered 7 asked

Let's find them! page 45

2 quacked 3 chirped 4 crowed 5 cackled 6 asked 7 replied

Let's go to the next step! page 46

1 "You are in my way," oinked the pig.
2 "I am off to round up sheep," barked the dog.
3 "Have you seen my mum?" quacked the duckling.
4 "I am hungry," mooed the cow.
5 "I just laid my first egg," clucked the hen.
6 "I am giving donkey rides today," brayed the donkey.

Let's aim high now! page 46

2 tweeted 3 neighed 4 brayed 5 oinked 6 squeaked 7 bleated

Let's put it together now! page 47

Saying verbs for people	Saying verbs for animals
whispered	bleated
agreed	hooted
replied	squeaked
shouted	cheeped
said	honked

Let's have a test! page 48

1 said
2 screamed
3 hooted
4 called
5 sang
6 told
7 "Do not come near the horse," said the vet.
8 We begged her to let us feed the hens.

Unit 9 Getting and giving

Let's find them! page 49

1 He couldn't ride his tricycle. 2 He felt sad. 3 Kim untied his parcel. 4 He forgot to be sad.

Let's go to the next step! page 50

2 gave 3 bought 4 saved 5 wrote 6 posted 7 pushed

Let's aim high now! page 50

2 He helped the boy.
3 I gave her a book.
4 Dad drove home.
5 The shop sold toys.
6 He has new shoes.
7 We gave her a present.

Let's find them! page 51

1 Firstly, we looked at home for things to give.
2 Our jumble sale opened at nine am.
3 We made $320 for Animal Rescue.
4 We all felt very pleased.

Let's go to the next step! page 52

2 won 3 posted 4 gave 5 shared 6 went 7 counted

Let's aim high now! page 52

1 The juggler hurt his foot.
2 We watched the magic show.
3 She bought six peaches.
4 I ate some banana cake.
5 Animal Rescue helps animals.
6 I liked the jugglers.

Let's put it together now! page 53

There are 9 simple sentences in this story.
1 Dad drove me to the shops. 2 He parked the car. 3 We bought some shopping. 4 We pushed our trolley to the car park. 5 Our car was gone! 6 Then I remembered something. 7 We had parked on the green level. 8 We were on the pink level. 9 Dad turned pink as well!

Let's have fun! page 53

- Sal put a band aid on her knee
- Scott took the dog for a walk
- I painted a poster
- Dad looked for his car
- He bandaged the dog's paw

Let's have a test! page 54

1 we
2 pushed
3 between cafe and I
4 between shop and He
5 saw
6 sells
7 They came to our jumble sale.
8 She drove home.

Unit 10 Doing things differently

Let's find them! page 55

1 My grandparents [Tuyen's] 2 Angelo
3 Our teacher 4 Kathy

Let's go to the next step! page 56

1 Birds 2 Dogs 3 Bees 4 Lions 5 Cats 6 Pigs

Let's aim high now! page 56

1 The dog gulped the dog food.
2 The goat chewed the straw.
3 The man milked the cow.
4 The rabbit nibbled the grass.
5 The cat drank the milk.

Let's find them! page 57

1 Ben 2 Huong 3 Timmy 4 Ben 5 The owner of the dim sum stall

Let's go to the next step! page 58

1 This kite 2 My brother 3 We 4 Suri
5 Stories 6 Bill and I

Let's aim high now! page 58

1 She made some noodles.
2 I bought a doner kebab.
3 We had yum cha today.
4 The cook made a stir fry.
5 They bought some fruit salad.
6 Dad cooked us spaghetti.

Let's put it together now! page 59

Cats and dogs

My dog chased a cat. The cat ran up a tree. It was stuck in the tree. Mum found a ladder. She helped the cat down safely. Our dog was in trouble. He was put in the dog house!

Let's have fun! page 59

1 The boy is eating an apple.
2 The girl is eating some noodles.
3 The dog is barking at the cat.
4 The cat is running up the tree.

Let's have a test! page 60

1 We love to eat sushi.
2 played
3 come
4 The flag has stars and stripes.
5 The dog barked loudly.
6 James
7 We
8 I

Unit 11 Telling stories

Let's find them! page 61

1 slowly 2 secretly 3 crossly 4 loudly 5 quickly

Let's go to the next step! page 62

1 greedily 2 secretly 3 crossly 4 loudly 5 swiftly
6 quickly

Let's aim high now! page 62

1 gently 2 bravely 3 quickly 4 gladly 5 snugly

Let's find them! page 63

2 bravely 3 rudely 4 angrily 5 Swiftly
6 quickly

Let's go to the next step! page 64

2 loudly 3 correctly 4 angrily 5 quickly
6 brightly

Let's aim high now! page 64

1 carefully 2 firmly 3 easily 4 smoothly
5 slowly 6 loudly

Let's put it together now page 65

The farmer crept quietly towards the rabbit. The rabbit pricked up his ears. Footsteps were coming slowly towards him. His burrow was nearby. He'd hop there as quickly as he could. Would he get there in time?

The farmer saw the rabbit move. He ran swiftly towards him. He was too late. The rabbit had made it safely home.

Let's have fun! page 65

- The eel frowned crossly.
- The kookaburras laughed happily.
- The emus danced crazily.
- The kangaroo nodded wisely.
- The rain fell heavily.

Let's have a test! page 66

1 kindly
2 clearly
3 slowly
4 easily
5 The eel spoke angrily.
6 Tiddalik laughed loudly.
7 The children listened quietly.
8 The kangaroo bravely chased the hunter.

Unit 12 Celebrating

Let's find them! page 67

1 on chairs and rugs
2 on their plate
3 after lunch
4 at once
5 in the afternoon

Let's go to the next step! page 68

1 She baked the birthday cake in the kitchen.
2 I bought her birthday present at the market.
3 Her party was held at the zoo.
4 She blew up the balloons outside the tent.
5 We put the strawberries on paper plates.
6 They went to the wedding.

Let's aim high now! page 68

1 The team practised before school.
2 The Book Fair is after the holidays.
3 They sang happy birthday after lunch.
4 We celebrated Chinese New Year after sunset.
5 Our term ends in two days.
6 My party will be on September 1st.

Let's find them! page 69

1 in the afternoon
2 at nine o'clock
3 in the back
4 inside the box
5 in the cupboard
6 into the box

Let's go to the next step! page 70

1 She blew up the balloons (before the party).
2 The party began (at two o'clock).
3 The party was (at her house).
4 We put the fruit (on the plates).
5 I hid her present (in the attic).

Let's aim high now! page 70

1 when 2 where 3 when 4 where 5 where
6 when

Let's put it together now! page 71

- The present is on the tree in picture number 2.
- The balloons are floating in the sky in picture number 5.
- The presents are under the tree in picture number 3.
- The cake is on the table in picture number 6.
- The cake is next to the glasses in picture number 1.
- The balloons are tied to the pole in picture number 4.

Let's have a test! page 72

1 at our house
2 by the water.
3 The picnic was in the park.
4 We played hide-and-seek near the house.
5 We had our picnic on the picnic rug.
6 The moon shone brightly.
7 He blew up the balloons after breakfast.
8 I went to the fête across the road.

Unit 13 Talking about time

Let's find them! page 73

1 "Don't you remember?"
2 "Is this present for me, Auntie Jean?"
3 "Will you teach me, please Dad?"
4 "Are you ready?"

Let's go to the next step! page 74

2 full stop 3 question mark 4 question mark
5 full stop 6 question mark 7 full stop

Let's aim high now! page 74

1 question 2 question 3 not a question
4 question 5 not a question 6 question

Let's find them! page 75

1 "A sundial tells the time."
2 "A shadow falls on its face."
3 "Yes, it has hours marked on its face."
4 "Yes, I'd like a digital watch, Grandpa."

Let's go to the next step! page 76

1 She is seven. How old is your sister?
2 He isn't hungry now. Why is he crying?
3 We don't have a sundial in our garden. Do you?
4 We have always lived here. Where do you live?
5 My grandpa has a pocket watch. Does yours?
6 I saw a water clock on TV. Have you seen one?

Let's aim high now! page 76

Questions	Answers
1 How many seconds are in a minute?	**1** There are 60 seconds in a minute.
2 How many minutes are in an hour?	**6** There are 12 months in a year.
3 How many hours are in a day?	**4** There are seven days in a week.
4 How many days are in a week?	**5** There are 52 weeks in a year.
5 How many weeks are in a year?	**7** There are four seasons in a year.
6 How many months are in a year?	**2** There are 60 minutes in an hour.
7 How many seasons are in a year?	**3** There are 24 hours in a day.

Let's put it together now! page 77

1 w				2 w	h	i	c	h		3 w	h	o
4 h	o	5 w		h						i		
e		h		a						l		
n		e		t						l		
		r										
6 a	r	e										

Let's have a test! page 78

1 What was your present? It was a cuckoo clock.
2 I know how to tell the time. Do you?
3 Who gave him his watch?
4 Are you going to be late?
5 Are there 60 minutes in an hour.
6 When is the party.
7 My Dad made a sundial.
8 There were dinosaurs in the past.

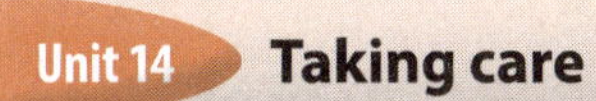

Unit 14 Taking care

Let's find them! page 79

2 Switch 3 Recycle 4 Put 5 Take 6 waste

Let's go to the next step! page 80

1 command 2 command 3 statement
5 command 6 statement 7 command

Let's aim high now! page 80

Statement	Command
1 He recycled his drink cans.	**5** Don't use plastic bags.
2 She put her litter in the bin.	**6** Walk to work to save fuel.
3 He recycled his mobile phone.	**2** Put litter in the bin.
4 He uses a worm farm to recycle waste.	**1** Recycle your drink cans.
5 We don't use plastic bags.	**7** Use a rainwater tank.
6 She walks to work to save fuel.	**3** Recycle your mobile phone.
7 They use a rainwater tank.	**4** Use a worm farm to recycle waste.

Let's find them! page 81

2 Be in bed by 8 pm.
3 You must return the forms tomorrow.
4 Pack them into your bags tonight.
6 Would you feed the cat too, please?
7 Will you take good care of Aunt Harriet?

Let's go to the next step? page 82

1 request 2 command 3 request 4 request
5 command 6 request

Let's aim high now! page 82

Command	Request
1 Eat your vegetables.	**4** Will you keep off the grass, please?
2 Take out the rubbish.	**6** Will you watch out for traffic, please?
3 Clean up that mess.	**7** Will you pass me the sauce, please?
4 Don't walk on the grass.	**3** Will you clean up that mess, please?
5 Clean your teeth.	**2** Will you take out the rubbish, please?
6 Watch out for traffic.	**5** Will you clean your teeth, please?
7 Pass the sauce.	**1** Will you eat your vegetables, please?

Let's put it together now! page 83

KEEP OFF THE G**RASS**
SAVE THE WH**ALE**S
KEEP AUS**TRALIA** BEAUTI**FUL**
BEWARE OF THE **DOG**
SAVE OUR P**LANE**T
WA**TCH** OUT F**OR** CYCL**ISTS**

Let's have a test! page 84

1. His room was always tidy.
2. Could you get me a 'No Junk Mail' sticker?
3. Put
4. Save
5. Recycle your plastic bags.
6. Do not enter.
7. Will you please recycle your paper?
8. Would you give up your seat, please?